CHEAP
EATS

SIMPLE, SUMPTUOUS MEALS FOR FOUR

YOU CAN MAKE FOR UNDER $10

Brooke Dojny and
Melanie Barnard

A JOHN BOSWELL ASSOCIATES/KING HILL PRODUCTIONS BOOK

HarperPerennial
A Division of HarperCollinsPublishers

This book is dedicated to Sue Mills.

HarperCollins books may be purchased for educational, business, or sales promotional use. For information, please write: Special Markets Department, HarperCollins Publishers, Inc., 10 East 53rd Street, New York, NY 10022.

FIRST EDITION
LIBRARY OF CONGRESS CATALOG CARD NUMBER 92-53400
ISBN 0-06-096617-3

93 94 95 96 97   10 9 8 7 6 5 4 3 2 1

Contents

◆

Introduction

❖

It is our opinion that eating is one of the great pleasures of life. Unlike some other special events, this one occurs at least three times a day, and it is a pleasure that we believe can be indulged within any budget. In fact, some of the best meals we have ever had have been the least expensive. Back in the sixties, when the "gourmet" revolution was at its peak, good food became synonymous with expensive (and rich and complicated) dishes. Today, however, people have come back to the delicious reality that a plate of perfectly cooked pasta with a garlicky clam sauce will win a lot more accolades than a tiny mound of fish eggs imported from halfway around the world.

In the great cuisines of the world, most of the best-loved and most often-requested dishes are those that are also among the least costly to prepare. Because the cooking of our own United States is now rightly placed in its own proud category, we have adapted some of our regional classics, including a real old-fashioned chicken pot pie, a maple- and mustard-flavored ham steak, all-American barbecued pork steaks, and a soothing corn and cheese chowder. We have updated some old favorites, too, such as macaroni and cheese (zipped up with chiles), baked beans (now a simply terrific main-dish soup), and fried chicken (it's just as crispy cooked our way, in the oven).

With nods to contemporary creativity, we have lots of colorful salads. Because we love the fact that people no longer believe that every single meal needs to include meat, we have created some delicious, hearty vegetarian menus. Armed with the knowledge that every good story is even better with a sweet ending, each of our menus finishes with a simple but satisfying dessert.

Our recipes also reflect the cooking and eating styles that have changed so rapidly in the last few years. These days, we want sophisticated yet streamlined recipes, low on fat and sugar and high on flavor, that can be prepared quickly. Actually the cook on a budget is right in line with these other lifestyle choices, because less expensive food is often healthier food—lighter in meat, stronger on fruits and vegetables, with a greater emphasis on complex carbohydrates. And when recipes are shortened to eliminate costly ingredients, preparation time is also speeded up.

While developing and testing the recipes in the book, we followed a few simple guidelines in order to stay under 10 dollars per menu. These guidelines also form the basis for our food shopping and cooking philosophy:

- Buy seasonal produce and regional cuts of meat
- Shop in volume when possible
- Use those coupons
- Choose quality in-house brands
- Avoid high-priced specialty ingredients
- Use the equipment you have on hand

Because it tastes best and costs least, we call for seasonal produce and have based our pricing accordingly. We have tried, where applicable, to suggest substitutions, so that you'll have some flexibility with a recipe when you shop for the ingredients.

All our menus were costed out on ingredients purchased at several supermarkets in Connecticut. Although we have made a concerted effort to err on the conservative (that is, expensive) side, there may be some individual items that cost a bit more in some regions. Overall, however, food costs will balance out, especially if you use in-season ingredients and shop intelligently.

When buying groceries, we suggest a commonsense approach based on the size of your family and their eating preferences. In general, larger packages offer a better buy. On the other hand, waste is costly. So if you find you're throwing out potatoes because they're sprouting green whiskers before you use them all, buy less. Unless there is an herb or spice you use with special frequency, buy these in small jars since their potency begins to deteriorate after a couple of months on the shelf. Our pricing of ice cream and frozen yogurt is based on buying the much more economical half-gallon size, which keeps well in the freezer for a couple of weeks. Also, for this book, we call for dried pasta, bought in one-pound packages.

In writing this book, a good deal of care was taken to avoid extremely hard-to-find ingredients or those that require side trips to specialty food stores. Similarly, the recipes were developed with much thought to the cookware and appliances available in the average kitchen. Standard-size pots and pans are called for, as are basic utensils, knives, and gadgets. Though some dishes can be made faster and easier with a food processor or microwave oven, alternative directions are always included.

With the exception of some baked desserts, which will keep for a couple of days, all the recipes in *Cheap Eats* serve four people. Ingredients listed as optional are truly that—without them the dish is still delicious and, they are, thus, not figured in the cost. Also, if a choice of ingredients is given, the first option is the one priced in the total.

Most important, though cooking tasty, satisfying food at an economical cost is the stated point of this book, our real goal was to provide enticing recipes and menus that are healthful and simple to prepare. It is our strong belief that everyone should be able to enjoy the real pleasures of the table. **Please note:** In the menus throughout this book, an asterisk after a dish indicates that recipe is included.

Spring

❖

No matter what the calendar says, depending upon where you live, spring may start as early as February or as late as April. For some, the beginning of this season of delicate renewal is ushered in with the first bloom of the crocus, but for a cook, it really begins with the sudden abundance of fresh asparagus. The season hits its stride when the cost of this delectable vegetable drops below $1.00 per pound (which is when we are likely to enjoy this favored delicacy for six or seven days running).

Asparagus may be the harbinger of the season, but strawberries and rhubarb, tender young greens and baby peas are close behind, pushing down produce prices and offering an exciting palate of flavors for the creative cook.

"Spring" lamb (really just young lamb) is now available year round, but tradition still favors it during this time of year, so it is often nicely priced at the market. Turkeys, hams, and eggs are popular around Easter, making them frequently featured items as well. Keep watch, for in this quickly changing season, prices vary greatly in just a week or two.

BRUNSWICK SOUP*

◆

CHEDDAR CHEESE BISCUITS*

◆

SPRING GREENS SALAD

◆

CHUNKY PEANUT BUTTER COOKIES*

◆

Brunswick soup takes its name from an old-fashioned American stew first made with squirrel and other small game. The original is claimed by several Southern counties by the name of Brunswick, but most likely the recipe comes from the American Indians, who often stewed together wild game and native vegetables, such as corn and okra. Cheddar cheese flecked biscuits extend the slightly Southern theme of this tasty, informal menu. Peanuts, another product of this part of the country, have become an all-American treat. The relatively new, but readily available "extra-chunky" peanut butter costs no more, but gives an especially nutty character to these delicious cookies.

BRUNSWICK SOUP

Makes 4 servings

This recipe is also good with leftover cooked chicken or turkey. Use canned chicken broth and simply add the cooked poultry at the end of the cooking time so that it will just heat through.

1 whole chicken (about 3½ pounds), cut up
1 medium onion, thinly sliced
1 celery rib, sliced
1 (16-ounce) can stewed tomatoes
1 cup frozen lima beans
1 cup frozen corn kernels
1 cup sliced okra (optional)
½ cup long-grain white rice
2 teaspoons dried thyme leaves
½ teaspoon salt
¼ teaspoon black pepper
2 to 3 teaspoons Worcestershire sauce to taste
¼ to ½ teaspoon hot pepper sauce to taste

1. Place the chicken (and giblets, if desired—but not the liver) in a large pot. Add the onion and celery and enough cold water to cover the chicken and vegetables. Bring to a boil, lower the heat, and simmer for 25 minutes, or until the chicken is tender and there is no trace of pink near the bone. Remove the chicken from the broth; reserve the broth. Let the chicken stand until cool enough to handle, and then remove the meat from the bones, discarding the skin and bones. Skim the fat from the broth. (The recipe can be prepared to this point up to a day ahead. Refrigerate the chicken and reserved broth separately. If made ahead, the fat will solidify and can be simply lifted off.)

2. Add the tomatoes, lima beans, corn, okra, rice, thyme, salt, and pepper to the broth. Simmer, partially covered, for 25 minutes, or until the rice is tender. Return the chicken to the soup and heat through, then season to taste with the Worcestershire sauce and hot pepper sauce.

CHEDDAR CHEESE BISCUITS

Makes 8 to 10 biscuits

Double the ingredients if you are having company.

    1 cup all-purpose flour
    2 teaspoons baking powder
    1½ teaspoons sugar
    ¼ teaspoon salt
    3 tablespoons solid vegetable shortening
    ⅓ cup grated Cheddar cheese
    ⅓ cup milk

1. Preheat the oven to 425 degrees.

2. In a mixing bowl, whisk or stir together the flour, baking powder, sugar, and salt. Using two knives or your fingers, cut or rub in the shortening until the mixture resembles coarse crumbs. Add the cheese, then the milk, stirring until the mixture comes together to form a soft dough.

3. Turn the dough out onto a lightly floured surface and knead 10 times. Roll or pat the dough to a ½ inch thickness, then cut with a 2-inch biscuit cutter. Reroll and cut the scraps. Place the biscuits about 2 inches apart on an un-

greased baking sheet. (Unbaked biscuits can be refrigerated for about 2 hours at this point.)

4. Bake for 10 to 12 minutes, until the biscuits are pale golden brown and well risen. Serve warm.

Chunky Peanut Butter Cookies

Makes about 40 cookies

> 1½ cups all-purpose flour
> ½ teaspoon baking soda
> ¼ teaspoon salt
> ¾ cup extra-chunky peanut butter
> ½ cup solid vegetable shortening or 8 tablespoons
>   (1 stick) softened butter
> ½ cup packed light brown sugar
> ½ cup granulated sugar
> 1 egg
> 1 teaspoon vanilla extract

1. Preheat the oven to 350 degrees. Lightly grease 1 or 2 large cookie sheets. Whisk or stir together the flour, baking soda, and salt.

(*continued on next page*)

(*continued*)

2. In a large mixing bowl, cream the peanut butter, shortening, brown sugar, and granulated sugar until smooth. Beat in the egg and vanilla. With the mixer on low speed, add the dry ingredients and mix until well blended.

3. Using a slightly rounded tablespoon of dough for each cookie, drop them about 2 inches apart on the prepared cookie sheets. Use a fork to make crisscross marks on top of each cookie and flatten them to about ½ inch thickness.

4. Bake for 12 to 15 minutes, until the cookies are lightly browned at the edges. Use a spatula to remove the cookies to a rack and let cool completely. Store in a tightly covered container up to 2 days or freeze for up to 1 month.

DILLED SALMON CAKES*

◆

TARTAR SAUCE

◆

SAUTÉED SUGAR SNAPS WITH WINE VINEGAR*

◆

CHOCOLATE FROZEN YOGURT

◆

Because it is an oilier fish than most, salmon (like tuna) takes very well to the canning process. And the canned variety is considerably less costly than the fresh. These salmon cakes stretch this flavorful fish even further by using it in combination with bread crumbs, eggs, and fresh herbs of the season. Serve with your favorite tartar sauce on the side. For a slightly uncommon vegetable, try sautéed sugar snap peas, if you're lucky enough to find them in your market. Sugar snaps are prepared by simply removing the stem ends and stringing them as you would a string bean. They're eaten pod and all, which makes them a good buy even if the per pound price looks a little elevated. Their taste is one of the real treats of the spring season. Finish the meal with scoops of chocolate frozen yogurt.

Dilled Salmon Cakes

Makes 4 servings

If you use fresh dill here, add a sprig to each plate as garnish. Serve with tartar sauce on the side.

 2 cups fresh white bread crumbs
 2 eggs, lightly beaten
 ½ cup minced scallions, including green tops
 2 teaspoons minced fresh dill or ½ teaspoon dried
 1 teaspoon lemon juice
 ¼ teaspoon black pepper
 1 (12-ounce) can salmon, drained
 2 tablespoons butter
 1 tablespoon vegetable oil

1. In a large mixing bowl, combine 1½ cups of the bread crumbs with the eggs, scallions, dill, lemon juice, and pepper and mix well. Add the salmon and mix with your hands, breaking the salmon into small pieces. (The recipe can be made to this point several hours ahead. Cover bowl with plastic wrap and refrigerate.)

2. Shape the salmon mixture into 8 patties, each about ½ inch thick. Place the remaining ½ cup of bread crumbs on a plate and dredge the salmon cakes in the crumbs to coat, patting them on so they adhere.

3. In a large skillet, melt the butter in the oil over medium heat. Add the salmon cakes and cook for about 3 minutes, until golden brown on the first side. Turn and cook for about 3 minutes on the second side, until browned on the bottom and steaming hot throughout.

4. Serve hot, with tartar sauce on the side.

SAUTÉED SUGAR SNAPS WITH WINE VINEGAR

Makes 4 servings

If sugar snaps don't appear in your market, you can substitute snow peas in this recipe, or simply serve fresh or frozen green peas.

1 pound sugar snap peas
2 tablespoons olive oil
1 tablespoon white wine vinegar
¼ teaspoon salt
⅛ teaspoon black pepper

1. Rinse the sugar snaps, drain, and pat dry on paper towels. Break off the stems and pull back to remove the strings.

2. Heat the oil in a large skillet. Add the sugar snaps and sauté them over medium-high heat, stirring frequently, for 4 to 5 minutes, until bright green and crisp-tender.

3. Remove the pan from the heat, add the vinegar, and stir to scrape up any browned bits from the bottom of the pan. Season with the salt and pepper and serve.

Ginger Turkey and Asparagus Stir-Fry*

◆

Brown or White Rice

◆

Sesame Popovers*

◆

Broiled Coconut Pineapple*

◆

One of the beauties of a stir-fry is that it is so adaptable to the ingredients that look best and are the cheapest on market day. Even at their everyday price, turkey breast cutlets are relatively inexpensive because they're pure protein, without any fat or waste. When they go on sale, they're a *real* bargain, so pick up a couple of packages for the freezer. In this dish, the turkey is sliced into strips, stir-fried with slender, diagonally cut asparagus, and seasoned with that compatible duo of fresh ginger and garlic. Serve the stir-fry over rice, and for a special treat, offer light, airy sesame-flavored popovers on the side. Fresh pineapple, sprinkled with coconut and run under the broiler, makes a terrific finale.

GINGER TURKEY AND
ASPARAGUS STIR-FRY

Makes 4 servings

1½ cups chicken broth
1 tablespoon soy sauce
1 tablespoon cornstarch
¼ teaspoon hot pepper flakes
1 pound boneless turkey breast cutlets
3 tablespoons vegetable oil
¾ pound asparagus, cut into 1-inch pieces
2 teaspoons minced fresh ginger
2 garlic cloves, minced
⅓ cup thinly sliced scallions, including green tops

1. In a 2-cup measuring cup or in a bowl, whisk together the chicken broth, soy sauce, cornstarch, and hot pepper. Set the sauce aside.

2. Cut the turkey into strips about ¼ inch wide and dry the meat thoroughly on paper towels.

3. Heat the oil in a large skillet or wok. When the oil is hot, add the turkey and cook over high heat, stirring almost

constantly, for about 2 minutes, until lightly browned. Add the asparagus and continue to cook, stirring, for 2 minutes.

4. Reduce the heat to medium. Add the ginger and garlic and cook for 1 minute. Stir the sauce mixture and pour it into the pan. Bring to a boil, stirring frequently, for 2 minutes, until the sauce is clear and thickened and the asparagus is crisp-tender. Stir in the scallions and serve.

Sesame Popovers

Makes 6 to 8 popovers

These can be made in popover pans, heatproof custard cups, or even muffin tins if they are the extra-large size.

    1 cup all-purpose flour
    ½ teaspoon salt
    1 cup milk
    1 tablespoon butter, melted
    2 eggs, lightly beaten
    1 tablespoon sesame seeds

(continued on next page)

(*continued*)

1. Preheat the oven to 450 degrees. Generously butter 6 popover tins, 8 (5-ounce) custard cups, or 8 deep muffin tins.

2. Sift the flour and the salt together into a medium bowl. Whisk in the milk, butter, and eggs until well blended. The batter will be thin, about the consistency of very thick cream. (The batter can be made several hours ahead. Stir before using.)

3. Divide the batter evenly among the pans, filling each no more than two-thirds full. Sprinkle the sesame seeds over the top of the batter in each tin.

4. Bake in the center of the preheated oven for 15 minutes. Reduce the heat to 350 degrees and continue to bake for 15 to 20 minutes, until the popovers are crisp and a rich golden brown. Serve at once.

BROILED COCONUT PINEAPPLE

Makes 4 servings

Cooking pineapple slightly helps to bring out its natural sweetness.

   3 tablespoons butter, melted
   8 thin slices of peeled fresh pineapple
   3 tablespoons brown sugar
   3 tablespoons shredded sweetened coconut

1. Preheat the broiler. Use a little of the butter to brush over the bottom of a shallow 1½-quart baking dish.

2. Arrange the pineapple slices slightly overlapping in the dish and sprinkle the brown sugar over the fruit. Drizzle the remaining melted butter on top. (The recipe can be made to this point several hours ahead.)

3. Broil the pineapple about 4 inches from the heat 2 to 3 minutes, until the topping is golden brown and bubbling. Sprinkle the coconut evenly over all and broil until the coconut is toasted, about 30 seconds. Serve warm

CANADIAN BACON WITH
CREAMY RED-EYE GRAVY*

◆

CORNMEAL WAFFLES*

◆

CHICORY SALAD WITH
CHIVE-HONEY DRESSING*

◆

CITRUS SHERBET

◆

While waffles are generally more expected at breakfast, they can also serve as a wonderful treat for supper—a welcome, and not at all uncommon, custom in the country. And these, made with cornmeal, go particularly well with Canadian bacon sautéed and topped with a variation on the Southern specialty called "red-eye gravy." In its true form, the gravy is made by frying some country ham and deglazing the pan with strong coffee. Here, cream is also added to smooth out the rough edges, but the essential taste is the same. Add a chicory salad tossed with a creamy chive-honey dressing, and a dish of refreshing citrus sherbet for dessert.

CANADIAN BACON WITH
CREAMY RED-EYE GRAVY

Makes 4 servings

You can really use any ham in this recipe. A smoked ham steak or even baked ham could be substituted for the Canadian bacon if you find a better value.

1 tablespoon butter
6 ounces Canadian bacon, sliced about ¼ inch thick
2 tablespoons brewed coffee (see Note)
½ cup whipping cream or heavy cream
⅛ teaspoon black pepper

1. Heat the butter in a large skillet. Add the Canadian bacon and cook over medium-high heat, turning once, until the edges are tinged with brown, about 2 minutes total.

2. Remove the bacon to a plate and pour the coffee into the skillet. Lower the heat to medium and stir up any browned bits from the bottom of the pan with a wooden spoon. Add the cream and simmer for about 2 minutes, until lightly thickened. Season with the pepper. To serve, spoon the gravy over the bacon.

(continued on next page)

(*continued*)

NOTE: Use strongly brewed coffee or ½ teaspoon instant coffee powder or granules dissolved in 2 tablespoons hot water.

CORNMEAL WAFFLES

Makes 4 servings

Essentially a cornbread batter made in a waffle iron, these come out crisp and light and crunchy.

   1 cup all-purpose flour
   1 cup yellow cornmeal
   1 tablespoon sugar
   1 tablespoon baking powder
   ¾ teaspoon salt
   2 eggs
   3 tablespoons vegetable oil
   1¼ cups milk

1. Preheat a waffle iron, greasing if necessary and following the manufacturer's instructions. Preheat the oven to 225 degrees.

2. For the waffles, stir together the flour, cornmeal, sugar, baking powder, and salt in a medium bowl.

3. In a small bowl, combine the eggs, oil, and milk. Whisk until well blended.

4. Pour the liquid ingredients over the flour mixture and stir just until the batter is blended and all the flour is moistened.

5. Using ¾ to 1 cup of batter for each waffle, make 4 waffles, following the instructions for your waffle iron. Cook until the steaming stops and the waffles are crisp and golden brown.

6. Remove to a baking sheet, cover loosely with foil, and keep warm in the preheated oven while you make the other waffles. Serve hot as soon as possible.

Chicory Salad with
Chive-Honey Dressing

Makes 4 servings

Sometimes called curly endive, this pretty, spiky green is best in spring when it's young and most tender. As an alternative, you can substitute young escarole or any other dark, slightly bitter green.

> 2 tablespoons red wine vinegar
> 1 teaspoon honey
> ¼ teaspoon salt
> ⅛ teaspoon black pepper
> ¼ cup vegetable oil
> 1 tablespoon mayonnaise
> 2 tablespoons minced chives
> 1 head of chicory, rinsed, dried, and torn into bite-
>   sized pieces

1. To make the dressing, combine the vinegar, honey, salt, and pepper in a small bowl. Whisk in the oil and the mayonnaise until smooth and well blended. Stir in the chives.

2. Place the chicory in a bowl, drizzle on the dressing, and toss to coat thoroughly.

FUSILLI WITH ARUGULA AND BACON*

◆

PLUM TOMATO SALAD*

◆

ITALIAN BREAD

◆

GLAZED STRAWBERRY SHORTCAKE TART *

◆

Arugula, which in the past was a rather pricey and exotic ingredient, is now much more readily available and thus more reasonably priced. It also grows easily. Like most "greens," it is at its peak of flavor and tenderness in the spring. If you have trouble finding arugula, this recipe is also very tasty made with fresh spinach. Add a bit more black pepper to simulate the "bite" from the arugula. Tossing lightly cooked arugula with bacon and pasta may sound avant-garde, but in some regions of Italy, this is a classic spring dish. When ripe tomatoes are not yet available locally, plum tomatoes are usually the best buy and also the tastiest in the market. Strawberries, the quintessential fruit of the season, are shown off to simple elegance in this lovely tart.

FUSILLI WITH ARUGULA AND BACON

Makes 4 servings

6 slices of bacon
1 pound fusilli
3 tablespoons olive oil
2 large garlic cloves, minced
4 cups arugula leaves or fresh spinach, thinly sliced
    crosswise
2/3 cup dry white wine
1/8 teaspoon salt
1/8 teaspoon black pepper
1/3 cup grated Parmesan cheese

1. In a large skillet, fry the bacon over medium heat, turning, until crisp. Drain on paper towels, crumble, and reserve. Pour off all but 2 tablespoons of the drippings in the skillet. (This can be done about 2 hours ahead.)

2. Cook the pasta in a large pot of boiling salted water for 9 to 10 minutes, or until *al dente*, tender but firm. Measure out and reserve 1/3 cup of the pasta cooking water. Drain well.

3. Meanwhile, heat the olive oil with the bacon drippings in the skillet. Add the garlic and cook for 30 seconds. Add the arugula and cook over medium heat, tossing to coat the arugula leaves with oil, for 1 minute. Continue to cook, stirring often, for 2 to 3 minutes longer, until the arugula leaves are wilted. Add the wine, salt, and pepper and simmer for 1 minute.

4. Toss the pasta with the sauce and reserved cooking water. Sprinkle on the Parmesan cheese and toss again. Sprinkle the crumbled bacon over the pasta and serve.

Plum Tomato Salad

Makes 4 servings

3 large plum tomatoes (about 12 ounces total)
1 sweet white or red onion
Salt and black pepper
2 tablespoons olive oil
2 teaspoons red wine vinegar

Slice the tomatoes and the onion about ¼ inch thick. Arrange in slightly overlapping slices on a serving platter or 4 plates. Season generously with salt and black pepper. Sprinkle the oil and vinegar over all.

GLAZED STRAWBERRY
SHORTCAKE TART

Makes 8 servings

SHORTCAKE CRUST
1 cup all-purpose flour
1 tablespoon sugar
1½ teaspoons baking powder
¼ teaspoon salt
5 tablespoons butter, cut into 8 pieces
¼ cup plus 2 tablespoons milk

FILLING
1 pint strawberries
½ cup strawberry jelly
1 tablespoon dry red or white wine or water
1 cup whipped cream (optional)

1. To make the shortcake crust, preheat the oven to 425 degrees. In a mixing bowl, whisk or stir together the flour, sugar, baking powder, and salt. Use your fingers or 2 knives to cut in the butter until the mixture resembles coarse meal. Add the milk and stir to make a soft dough.

2. Using floured hands, turn the dough out onto a lightly floured surface and knead 6 to 8 times, until smooth. Press the dough into a 9-inch tart pan or pie plate, pressing the sides above the rim and fluting the edges if using a pie plate.

3. Bake the shortcake crust for 8 to 10 minutes, until golden brown. The tart shell will puff somewhat during baking, but prick the bottom with a fork if it puffs up unevenly. Let the shell cool at least 10 minutes before filling; it should be slightly warm when the berries are added so that some of the berry juices can permeate the shortcake crust.

4. To fill the tart shell, hull the berries, then cut each in several slices from point to hull. Arrange the slices, overlapping, to completely cover the bottom of the tart shell.

5. In a small nonaluminum saucepan, heat the jelly with the wine just until the jelly melts. Brush the warm glaze generously over the berries.

6. Refrigerate the tart at least 30 minutes or up to 4 hours before serving. Add a dollop of whipped cream to each serving, if desired.

ROASTED PARMESAN POTATOES*

◆

CHICKEN WITH
GARLIC VINEGAR SAUCE*

◆

STEAMED ASPARAGUS

◆

LEMON CUSTARD MOUSSE*

◆

This is an easy-to-make, but absolutely stunning dinner for family or special guests. The chicken and the potatoes are inspired by the gutsy, delicious food served in romantic French bistros. Steamed asparagus is perhaps one of the most elegant—and economical—fresh vegetables in the spring market and is, in fact, considered to be a celebratory seasonal main course in parts of Europe. Next to chocolate, lemon is probably the world's second most favorite dessert flavor. This rich, smooth, slightly tart mousse will certainly further its popularity.

ROASTED PARMESAN POTATOES

Makes 4 servings

These savory potatoes are particularly nice as an accompaniment to the Chicken with Garlic Vinegar Sauce, which follows.

 1½ **pounds small red potatoes**
 3 tablespoons olive oil
 ¼ **teaspoon salt**
 ¼ **teaspoon black pepper**
 2 tablespoons grated Parmesan cheese

1. Preheat the oven to 425 degrees. Halve or quarter the potatoes so that they are in approximately 1½-inch chunks. Place the potatoes on a 10-by-15-inch jelly-roll pan. Drizzle on the oil, sprinkle with the salt and pepper, and toss to coat completely. Spread the potatoes out to make a single layer.

2. Bake for 20 minutes. Turn the potatoes with a spatula and sprinkle the cheese over them. Bake for about 20 minutes longer, until the potato chunks are golden brown and tender when pierced with a fork.

CHICKEN WITH GARLIC VINEGAR SAUCE

Makes 4 servings

2½ to 3 pounds cut-up chicken parts
¼ teaspoon salt
¼ teaspoon black pepper
2 tablespoons olive oil
3 garlic cloves, minced
½ teaspoon dried thyme leaves
½ teaspoon dried rosemary
3 tablespoons red wine vinegar
1 (16-ounce) can stewed tomatoes, with their juices

1. Season the chicken with the salt and pepper. Heat the oil in a large skillet. Add the chicken and sauté over medium-high heat, turning, for about 10 minutes, or until browned all over. Use tongs to remove the chicken to a plate. Pour off all but 1 tablespoon drippings.

2. Add the garlic, thyme, and rosemary to the skillet and cook over low heat for 1 minute, stirring constantly to prevent the garlic from burning. Add the vinegar and simmer,

stirring, for 2 minutes. Add the tomatoes and their juices, breaking up large chunks of tomatoes with the back of a spoon.

3. Return the chicken to the skillet, skin side up; also add any juices that have accumulated on the plate. Partially cover the pan and simmer over low heat for 10 minutes. Uncover and simmer 5 to 8 minutes longer, until the chicken is cooked through with no trace of pink near the bone, and the sauce is slightly reduced and thickened. Spoon off any excess fat that may have risen to the surface. Taste and season with additional salt and pepper if needed.

LEMON CUSTARD MOUSSE

Makes 4 servings

> **2 whole eggs**
> **2 egg yolks**
> **¾ cup sugar**
> **⅓ cup lemon juice**
> **2 teaspoons grated lemon zest**
> **2 tablespoons butter**
> **½ cup whipping cream or heavy cream**
> **⅛ teaspoon grated nutmeg**

1. In a heavy medium saucepan, whisk together the eggs, egg yolks, and sugar until very well blended and lightly thickened. Whisk in the lemon juice and lemon zest. Add the butter. Set the pan over low heat and cook, stirring constantly, for 6 to 8 minutes, until the custard thickens and barely comes to a boil. Immediately scrape the custard into a bowl. Cover and refrigerate the lemon curd for at least 6 hours or up to 24 hours until well chilled.

2. Whip the cream, then fold it into the chilled lemon curd. Spoon into 4 individual dessert dishes or into an attractive serving bowl. Sprinkle the nutmeg over the top. Serve immediately or refrigerate for up to 4 hours before serving.

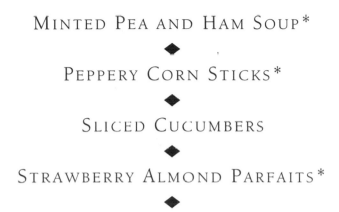

MINTED PEA AND HAM SOUP*

◆

PEPPERY CORN STICKS*

◆

SLICED CUCUMBERS

◆

STRAWBERRY ALMOND PARFAITS*

◆

This beautiful green pea soup is made substantial by the addition of potatoes and is flavored with the salty tang of smoked ham and the refreshing taste of mint. If you happen to own corn-stick pans—cast-iron molds that make cornbread in the shape of ears of corn—use them to make corn sticks to go with this soup. Otherwise, directions are given to turn the same peppery batter into cornbread. Crisp sliced cucumbers are good on the side, and a dessert of strawberry parfaits topped with toasted almonds completes the meal with a seasonal flourish.

MINTED PEA AND HAM SOUP

Makes 4 servings

1 tablespoon butter
1 large onion, coarsely chopped
¾ pound all-purpose potatoes (2 large), peeled and
    thinly sliced
4 cups chicken broth
2 cups frozen green peas, thawed
3 tablespoons chopped fresh mint or 1½ teaspoons
    dried
1½ cups half-and-half or light cream
¼ pound smoked or baked ham, cut into small dice
¼ teaspoon black pepper
⅛ teaspoon salt
⅛ teaspoon hot pepper sauce

1. Heat the butter in a large saucepan or soup pot. Add the
onion and cook over medium heat, stirring occasionally, for
5 minutes, until softened. Add the potatoes and chicken
broth. Bring to a simmer, reduce the heat to low, cover, and
cook for 10 minutes. Add the peas and simmer, uncovered,
for 8 minutes, or until the potatoes and the peas are tender.
Stir in the mint.

2. Puree the soup, in batches if necessary, in a food processor or blender. Return the soup to the pot and add the half-and-half and the ham. If the soup is too thick, add up to 1 cup of water.

3. Bring the soup to a simmer and season with the pepper, salt, and hot sauce.

PEPPERY CORN STICKS

Makes about 14 corn sticks

You can also bake this cornbread batter in a 9-inch square pan or 9-inch cast-iron skillet for about 18 minutes.

   1 cup yellow or white cornmeal
   1 cup all-purpose flour
   2 tablespoons sugar
   4 teaspoons baking powder
   ¾ teaspoon salt
   ½ teaspoon black pepper
   1 egg
   1 cup milk
   ¼ cup vegetable oil

(*continued on next page*)

(*continued*)

1. Preheat the oven to 425 degrees. Grease 14 corn-stick molds with vegetable oil.

2. In a medium bowl, stir or whisk together the cornmeal, flour, sugar, baking powder, salt, and pepper.

3. In a small bowl, whisk together the egg, milk, and oil.

4. Pour the liquids into the flour mixture and stir just until the batter is blended and the flour is moistened.

5. Place the corn-stick molds in the oven to heat for 5 minutes. Remove with pot holders and fill the molds with the batter, spreading it so that it fills the molds evenly.

6. Return the molds to the oven and bake for 9 to 12 minutes, until the corn sticks are cooked through and lightly browned on top.

7. Remove the corn sticks from their molds with a small knife and serve warm.

Strawberry Almond Parfaits

Makes 4 servings

¼ cup slivered or sliced almonds
1 pint strawberries
3 tablespoons sugar
1 teaspoon lemon juice
1 pint vanilla ice cream or frozen yogurt

1. Preheat the oven to 350 degrees. Spread the almonds out in an even layer in a pie pan and toast them for about 8 minutes, stirring once, until the nuts are a rich golden brown. Chop the almonds quite fine and set aside.

2. Hull the strawberries. Mash half the berries in a bowl with the sugar and lemon juice or puree in a food processor. Slice the remaining berries and combine with the puree.

3. Place a small scoop of ice cream in each of 4 stemmed dessert dishes. Spoon on half the berry sauce. Top with another scoop of ice cream and spoon on the remaining sauce. Sprinkle the toasted almonds over the parfaits.

YELLOW RICE AND PEAS*

◆

CUBAN-STYLE BLACK BEANS*

◆

SWEET AND HOT PEPPER RELISH*

◆

TROPICAL FRUIT PLATTER

◆

This meatless meal, which all your vegetarian friends will love, is one variation on the staple diet of many peoples in the Caribbean and Latin America—and indeed in many other countries of the world. Black beans, with their firm texture and attractive shine, are especially appealing because they hold their shape well when cooked. Serve the flavorful, slightly soupy beans spooned alongside the brilliant yellow rice, and sprinkle the sweet-hot relish over both. If you'd like, offer toasted Cuban or French bread with the meal. And this entire meal falls so far below the ten dollar limit that any full-time meat eaters can be accommodated with a piece of grilled or broiled chicken, sausage, or ham steak.

A platter of tropical fruits is a welcome dessert. Choose from papayas, mangoes, bananas, pineapple, selecting whatever looks best and costs least.

Yellow Rice and Peas

Makes 4 servings

Either regular long-grain or "converted" rice works well in this recipe. The brilliant yellow color is achieved by using turmeric, a spice used often in Indian cooking.

2 tablespoons olive oil
1 medium onion, chopped
¾ teaspoon turmeric
1¼ cups long-grain white rice
¾ cup frozen green peas, thawed
¾ teaspoon salt
⅛ teaspoon black pepper

1. In a medium saucepan, heat the oil. Add the onion and cook over medium heat, until softened, about 3 minutes. Add the turmeric and the rice and cook, stirring, until the rice is coated with oil and slightly opaque, about 2 minutes. Add 2½ cups of water, bring to a simmer, reduce the heat to very low, cover, and cook for 15 minutes.

2. Stir in the peas and the salt and pepper. Cook, covered, for 5 minutes, or until the rice and peas are tender and the liquid is absorbed.

CUBAN-STYLE BLACK BEANS

Makes 4 servings

If you have time, you can trim your budget even more by soaking and cooking dried black beans according to the package directions.

    ¼ cup olive oil
    1 large onion, coarsely chopped
    2 garlic cloves, minced
    2 teaspoons chili powder
    2 (15- to 16-ounce) cans black beans, rinsed and
        drained
    Pinch of sugar
    1 bay leaf, broken in half
    2 teaspoons cider vinegar
    ¼ teaspoon salt
    ⅛ teaspoon black pepper
    ½ teaspoon hot pepper sauce

1. Heat the oil in a large saucepan. Add the onion and garlic and cook for 2 minutes over medium heat. Stir in the chili powder and cook, stirring, for 1 minute.

2. Add the beans, sugar, bay leaf, and 3 cups of water. Simmer over low heat, uncovered, for 15 minutes. Season with vinegar, salt, pepper, and hot pepper sauce. The beans should be somewhat soupy. If too thick, add additional water. If too thin, simmer, uncovered, for a few more minutes to thicken.

3. Discard the pieces of bay leaf and serve the beans with rice.

SWEET AND HOT PEPPER RELISH

Makes about 2 cups

This zesty condiment is also terrific with broiled hamburgers or cold chicken. The Vidalia onion, or another sweet, mild spring onion, is wonderful in this relish.

 1 small red pepper
 ¾ cup chopped red onion or sweet yellow onion
 1 to 2 jalapeño peppers, seeded and minced
 ½ teaspoon lemon or lime juice
 ¼ teaspoon salt

1. Remove the ribs and seeds from the red pepper and chop quite fine.

2. In a small bowl, combine the chopped red pepper with the onion and jalapeño. Stir in the lemon juice and salt.

3. Cover and refrigerate for at least 30 minutes, or for up to several hours, to allow the flavors to blend.

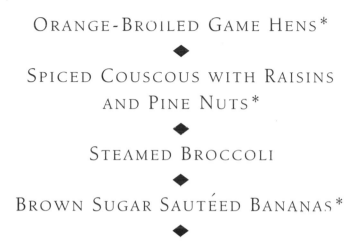

ORANGE-BROILED GAME HENS*

SPICED COUSCOUS WITH RAISINS
AND PINE NUTS*

STEAMED BROCCOLI

BROWN SUGAR SAUTÉED BANANAS*

More and more people are discovering couscous, the tiny
Moroccan semolina pasta that cooks by simply steeping in
boiling water for a few minutes. Here it's combined with
sweet and hot spices, raisins, and pine nuts to create a dish
with a slightly Middle Eastern air. The spicy couscous goes
beautifully with game hens that are burnished with a tangy
marmalade-based glaze, and spears of bright green
broccoli. Bananas, when sautéed in a simple butter and
brown sugar syrup, are transformed into being meltingly
tender inside, but with a sweetly caramelized, almost
crackly glaze outside. Finished with a spoonful of tart,
refreshing yogurt, the result is a perfect interplay of flavor
and texture.

ORANGE-BROILED GAME HENS

Makes 4 servings

This easy glaze is wonderful on chicken and turkey, too.

  2 Cornish game hens, about 1½ pounds each
  4 teaspoons olive oil
  2 tablespoons orange marmalade
  ¼ teaspoon curry powder
  1 teaspoon vinegar (any type)
  ½ teaspoon salt
  ¼ teaspoon black pepper

1. Preheat the broiler. Cut the hens in half, using either a cleaver or poultry shears, cutting around and discarding the backbones. Use the palm of your hand to flatten the halves slightly.

2. To make the glaze, combine 2 teaspoons of the oil with the marmalade and curry powder in a small saucepan. Cook over medium heat, stirring, until the marmalade is melted, about 1 minute. Or heat in a small glass dish in a microwave oven. Stir in the vinegar.

3. Brush or rub the hens with the remaining 2 teaspoons oil and season with the salt and pepper. Place the hen halves, skin side down, on a broiler pan and broil about 5 inches from the heat source for 10 minutes.

4. Brush the hens with the glaze. Turn skin side up and broil for 5 minutes. Brush liberally with glaze and continue to broil for about 5 minutes longer, until the thigh meat juices run clear when pierced with a knife and the skin is nicely browned.

Spiced Couscous with Raisins and Pine Nuts

Makes 4 servings

If pine nuts aren't readily available in your supermarket, use slivered almonds instead.

   2 tablespoon olive oil
   2 tablespoons pine nuts (pignoli)
   ½ cup raisins
   1 garlic clove, minced
   ½ teaspoon ground cinnamon
   ¼ teaspoon ground allspice
   ⅛ teaspoon cayenne
   1½ cups packaged couscous
   2 cups boiling water
   ¾ teaspoon salt

1. In a medium saucepan, heat the oil. Add the pine nuts and cook over low heat, stirring, until the nuts are golden brown, about 2 minutes. Add the raisins, garlic, cinnamon, allspice, and cayenne. Cook, stirring, for 1 minute.

2. Add the couscous to the saucepan, along with the 2 cups of boiling water and the salt. Stir once with a fork, cover tightly, and remove from the heat. Let stand, covered, for 5 minutes.

3. Stir with a fork before serving to fluff the couscous and combine the other ingredients. (This recipe can be made up to a day ahead and reheated over very low heat or in a microwave oven.)

BROWN SUGAR SAUTÉED BANANAS

Makes 4 servings

   3 large or 4 small firm but ripe bananas (about
       1½ pounds)
   2½ tablespoons butter
   2½ tablespoons brown sugar
   ¼ teaspoon grated nutmeg
   ½ cup vanilla yogurt

1. Peel the bananas and cut them into long diagonal slices about ½ inch thick.

2. In a large skillet, cook the butter and brown sugar over medium heat, stirring, until the sugar dissolves. Place the bananas in the syrup in a single layer, reduce the heat to medium-low, and cook for 3 to 4 minutes, until browned on the first side. Turn with a small spatula or tongs and cook on the second side until the bananas are soft and richly browned.

3. Arrange on dessert plates, sprinkle with the nutmeg, and serve warm, topped with spoonfuls of yogurt.

HERBED AND SPICED
VEAL MEATBALLS*

◆

LEMON-PARSLEY FETTUCCINE*

◆

STEAMED ZUCCHINI AND
YELLOW SQUASH

◆

SOUR CREAM
CHOCOLATE COOKIES*

◆

This menu is an upscale, contemporary twist on favorite family foods. Meatballs are always a top choice by kids of all ages, but their parents will also love these well-seasoned ones made with veal. Pasta, which used to be called spaghetti, is one of everyone's best-liked starches. Flavored up with little more than some lemon and chopped parsley, this makes a delightful accompaniment to the spicy meatballs. Colorful squashes are both economical and simple to cook. Chocolate cookies will disappear fast, especially these that are enriched with the tang of sour cream.

HERBED AND SPICED VEAL MEATBALLS

Makes 4 servings

Ground veal is a tasty and lower-fat hamburger alternative. It is also a relatively inexpensive way to enjoy this delicate meat. If ground veal is too expensive in your market, ground turkey—always a best buy—makes an excellent substitute.

1 pound ground veal or ground turkey
¾ cup fresh bread crumbs
1 egg
1 small onion, minced
½ teaspoon dried thyme
¼ teaspoon grated nutmeg
¼ teaspoon ground allspice
¼ teaspoon salt
¼ teaspoon black pepper
Pinch of ground cloves
1½ tablespoons vegetable oil
½ cup chicken broth
⅓ cup dry white wine

1. In a large bowl, use your hands to mix together the veal, bread crumbs, egg, onion, thyme, nutmeg, allspice, salt, pepper, and cloves. Form into 16 balls, each 1 to 1½ inches in diameter.

2. In a large skillet, heat the oil. Add the meatballs and cook over medium heat, turning often with tongs or a spatula, for 13 to 15 minutes, or until browned and cooked through. Add the broth and wine to the skillet and simmer, stirring often and scraping up browned bits clinging to the bottom of the pan, for 2 minutes, or until the sauce is lightly reduced. Serve the meatballs with the sauce.

LEMON-PARSLEY FETTUCCINE

Makes 4 side-dish servings

Add a 6-ounce can of tuna to this and you will have a lovely main course for two. If you have chicken broth on hand, use it in place of the water.

8 ounces fettuccine
3 tablespoons olive oil
1 garlic clove, minced
1 tablespoon lemon juice
½ teaspoon grated lemon zest
¼ teaspoon black pepper
3 tablespoons chopped parsley
Salt

1. Cook the fettuccine in a large pot of boiling salted water for 9 to 10 minutes, until *al dente,* tender but firm. Drain.

2. Heat the oil in a small saucepan. Add the garlic and cook over medium-low heat for 1 minute. Stir in the lemon juice, lemon zest, pepper, and 2 tablespoons of water.

3. Toss the sauce with the pasta. Add the parsley, season with salt to taste, toss again, and serve.

SOUR CREAM CHOCOLATE COOKIES

Makes about 4 dozen cookies

Extra cookies can be stored airtight for a few days or frozen for a snack or dessert another time.

1½ ounces unsweetened chocolate
1½ cups all-purpose flour
1½ teaspoons baking powder
¼ teaspoon baking soda
¼ teaspoon salt
8 tablespoons (1 stick) butter, softened
1 cup sugar
1 egg
½ cup sour cream
1 teaspoon vanilla extract

1. Melt the chocolate in a small pan set over hot water or in a microwave oven. Sift or whisk together the flour, baking powder, baking soda, and salt. Set aside.

(*continued on next page*)

(*continued*)

2. In the bowl of an electric mixer, cream together the butter and sugar until light. Beat in the egg, then the sour cream and vanilla until smooth. With the mixer on low speed, blend in the flour mixture. Refrigerate the dough for at least 1 hour or up to 24 hours before baking.

3. Preheat the oven to 375 degrees. Lightly grease 2 large cookie sheets. Drop the dough by heaping teaspoons onto the prepared cookie sheets, leaving 2 inches to allow for spreading.

4. Bake for 10 to 12 minutes, until the cookies are lightly rounded and set. Use a spatula to remove the cookies to a rack and let cool completely. (Store airtight for up to 3 days or freeze up to 1 month.)

Summer

♦

Summertime is probably the next best thing to heaven for people who love to cook and to eat. Whether you have your own vegetable garden, fruit trees, and berry patch or you do your harvesting at the local produce stand, this is the season to savor the luscious edible gifts from the earth at their best prices and peak flavor. Though the specialties of the week may vary according to the area of the country in which you live, keep an eye out for the most economical opportunities to enjoy luscious ripe peaches and blushing nectarines, juicy plums and sweet cherries, dusky melons, and colorful berries. Zucchini and all manner of summer squash abound now as do eggplants, peppers, and those two crown jewels of summer—native corn and homegrown tomatoes.

And because as a nation we are hooked on grilling out, the ground meats, pork steaks, chicken, and even steaks so suitable for the backyard barbecue are often placed on summer special at the supermarket. In addition to having all this bounty available at good prices and peak taste, the fruits, vegetables, and meats of this season need very little in the way of kitchen preparation—a real bonus to the cook in hot weather.

MOLASSES AND MUSTARD GRILLED CHICKEN*

◆

PICNIC POTATO SALAD*

◆

SLICED BEEFSTEAK TOMATOES

◆

BLUEBERRY COBBLER*

◆

Barbecued chicken, potato salad, thick and juicy ripe tomato slices, and sweet blueberry cobbler are components of perhaps the quintessential American summer meal. It's an added bonus that all these delicious dishes are so easy to prepare—and so economical in season.

Choose chicken parts that are on sale that week or buy a whole bird and cut it up yourself. You can marinate the chicken and make the potato salad a few hours ahead. Waxy potatoes are best for salad since they hold their shape better after cooking than do russet potatoes. All-purpose potatoes can be used, but cook them just until tender so they don't fall apart. Bake the cobbler before dinner so it will still be a bit warm at serving time. The tomatoes should, of course, be the ripest you can find.

Molasses and Mustard Grilled Chicken

Makes 4 servings

⅓ cup molasses
3 tablespoons cider vinegar
1½ tablespoons grainy or Dijon mustard
1½ tablespoons vegetable oil
2 teaspoons Worcestershire sauce
⅛ teaspoon salt
⅛ teaspoon black pepper
3 pounds cut-up chicken parts

1. In a shallow dish large enough to hold the chicken in a single layer, stir together the molasses, vinegar, mustard, oil, Worcestershire, salt, and black pepper. Add the chicken, turning to coat all sides. Cover and marinate in the refrigerator for 2 to 3 hours, turning 3 or 4 times.

(*continued on next page*)

(*continued*)

2. Build a medium-hot barbecue fire. Remove the chicken from the marinade, but reserve the marinade. Grill the chicken, skin side down, for about 5 minutes. Brush with some of the reserved marinade, turn, and grill another 5 minutes. Continue to grill, brushing with the marinade and turning occasionally, until 2 minutes before the chicken is done, for a total cooking time of 25 minutes for the light meat and 30 minutes for the dark meat. The chicken is done when the skin is lightly charred and the juices run clear when the flesh is pierced with a sharp knife tip or a skewer. Serve warm or at room temperature.

PICNIC POTATO SALAD

Makes 4 servings

1½ pounds red or yellow waxy or all-purpose
    potatoes, unpeeled and cut into 2-inch chunks
2 tablespoons cider or white wine vinegar
2 tablespoons vegetable or olive oil
½ teaspoon salt
¼ teaspoon black pepper
⅓ cup thinly sliced celery
⅓ cup thinly sliced scallions with their green tops
⅔ cup mayonnaise
1 tablespoon Dijon mustard
1½ tablespoons milk
⅛ teaspoon paprika

1. Cook the unpeeled potato chunks in a large saucepan of boiling salted water until just fork-tender, 15 to 20 minutes. Drain well. Leave the skins on or peel the potatoes, as you prefer. Cut the potatoes into rough ½-inch cubes and put them in a medium bowl. Sprinkle on the vinegar, oil, salt, and pepper and toss with the warm potatoes. Let stand about 15 minutes to cool and absorb the liquid.

(*continued on next page*)

(*continued*)

2. Add the celery and scallions to the potatoes. In a small bowl, combine the mayonnaise, mustard, and milk. Stir to blend well. Add to the potatoes and toss gently but thoroughly to coat. Cover and chill at least 30 minutes, or up to 6 hours before serving.

3. At serving time, taste and add more salt and pepper as needed. Gently stir the salad again, then sprinkle the paprika over the top for garnish.

BLUEBERRY COBBLER

Makes 4 servings

You can even use frozen berries here. Just rinse off any ice crystals and pat the berries dry between layers of paper towels.

3 cups blueberries
½ cup sugar
½ teaspoon grated lemon zest
¼ teaspoon ground cinnamon
2 teaspoons lemon juice
1 teaspoon vanilla extract

1 tablespoon butter
1 cup all-purpose flour
1 tablespoon sugar
2 teaspoons baking powder
½ teaspoon salt
2 tablespoons butter
⅓ cup whipping cream or heavy cream

1. Preheat the oven to 425 degrees. In a mixing bowl, toss together the blueberries, sugar, lemon zest, cinnamon, lemon juice, and vanilla. Place the fruit in a 9-inch glass pie plate. Dot with the butter.

2. For the dough, combine the flour, 2 teaspoons sugar, the baking powder, and the salt in a mixing bowl. Blend well. Cut the butter into bits and rub into the flour with your fingertips until the mixture resembles coarse meal. Stir in the cream just until the dough comes together. Turn onto a lightly floured surface and knead 8 times. Roll or pat into an 8½-inch round. Trim the edges and crimp lightly with a fork. Set the dough over the fruit. Cut several slashes in the dough as steam vents. Sprinkle the remaining 1 teaspoon sugar over the top.

3. Bake 20 to 25 minutes, until the crust is golden brown and the fruit is tender. Let cool on a rack, but serve warm or at room temperature within 3 or 4 hours of baking.

LINGUINE TONNATO *

◆

ARUGULA AND
GORGONZOLA SALAD *

◆

BREAD STICKS

◆

STRAWBERRIES TOSSED WITH
STRAWBERRY VINEGAR

◆

Full of sunny Mediterranean flavors, this menu is sort of like a mini-vacation on the Italian Riviera. The pasta dish is reminiscent of the flavors of the classic creamy tuna sauce of that region. Even the most finicky of fish-haters seems to like canned tuna, and with lots of garlic and herbs, it is a guaranteed winner. Arugula is a rather pricey little treat, but its pungent flavor goes a long way, so depending on its price, combine it with other seasonal greens to keep to the budget.

Fruit vinegars used to be hard to find, but now most large supermarkets carry them. A splash of the lightly sweet/sour flavor is a surprisingly delicious accent for very ripe strawberries. Raspberry vinegar can also be used. Serve the berries with a bowl of confectioners' sugar on the side for dipping.

Linguine Tonnato

Makes 4 servings

1 pound linguine
¼ cup plus 2 tablespoons olive oil
1 large green bell pepper, chopped
1 large onion, chopped
2 garlic cloves, minced
1 teaspoon dried oregano
½ teaspoon dried basil
¼ teaspoon hot pepper flakes
1 (16-ounce) can plum tomatoes, with their juices
3 tablespoons thinly sliced black olives
1 (12-ounce) can tuna in oil or water, drained and
    broken into chunks
Salt and black pepper

(*continued on next page*)

(*continued*)

1. Cook the linguine in a large pot of boiling salted water until it is *al dente,* tender but firm, 9 to 10 minutes. Drain well.

2. While the pasta cooks, heat the oil in a large skillet. Add the green pepper, onion, and garlic and cook over medium-low heat for about 5 minutes, until softened. Stir in the oregano, basil, hot pepper, and tomatoes with their juices. Bring to a simmer, stirring and breaking up the tomatoes with the back of a spoon. Stir in the olives. Simmer for 5 minutes.

3. Toss the pasta with the sauce, then toss gently with the tuna until combined. Taste and add salt and pepper as desired.

ARUGULA AND GORGONZOLA SALAD

Makes 4 servings

Arugula is very potent in flavor, so it is often used as an accent and mixed with other greens, such as romaine or leaf lettuce. Any blue-veined cheese can be used in place of the Gorgonzola.

2 tablespoons red wine vinegar
¾ teaspoon Dijon mustard
⅛ teaspoon salt
⅛ teaspoon black pepper
¼ cup plus 2 tablespoons olive oil
1 small head of leaf lettuce or ½ head of romaine
1 small bunch of arugula
¼ cup crumbled Gorgonzola cheese

1. To make the vinaigrette, combine the vinegar, mustard, salt, and pepper in a small bowl. Whisk in the olive oil. Taste and add additional salt and pepper as desired, but go lightly on the salt because the cheese is salty.

2. To make the salad, rinse, dry, and tear the lettuce and arugula into bite-sized pieces. In a salad bowl, toss the greens with the dressing, then toss again with the cheese.

SPICED GRILLED LAMB PATTIES*

◆

PITA BREADS

◆

TOMATO AND CUCUMBER SALAD WITH YOGURT CREAM*

◆

ANISE POACHED APRICOTS*

◆

Though there is a touch of the exotic in this menu, the ingredients are readily available and the dishes are simple to prepare. Grilling is a wonderful way to cook lamb, and these assertively spiced ground lamb patties are especially tasty. Wrap the pita breads in foil, then heat them at the side of the grill while the lamb is cooking. The pitas and the salad can accompany the lamb, but you can also build a "burger" by stuffing the lamb patties into the pita "pockets," then spooning in some of the salad. Apricots have a short season, but these luscious fruits are well worth highlighting when you can find them.

Spiced Grilled Lamb Patties

Makes 4 servings

1½ pounds ground lamb
1 large onion, chopped
½ cup fresh bread crumbs
2 garlic cloves, minced
3 tablespoons chopped fresh mint or 1½ teaspoons
    dried
1½ teaspoons ground cumin
½ teaspoon ground coriander
1 teaspoon salt
1 teaspoon black pepper

1. Light a medium-hot fire in your barbecue grill.

2. In a medium bowl, combine all the ingredients, working
the mixture together gently with your hands. Shape into 4
large patties, each about ½ inch thick. (The patties can be
made several hours ahead and refrigerated.)

3. Grill the lamb patties, turning once, for about 5 minutes
per side, until nicely charred on the outside, but with a hint
of pink in the middle.

TOMATO AND CUCUMBER SALAD WITH YOGURT CREAM

Makes 4 servings

This salad, much like a relish, is best made an hour or two ahead to allow the flavors to meld.

1 cucumber
2 ripe tomatoes
⅔ cup plain yogurt
3 tablespoons minced onion
1 tablespoon chopped fresh mint or ½ teaspoon dried
1 tablespoon milk
½ teaspoon salt
¼ teaspoon black pepper

1. Peel the cucumber. Seed the cucumber and the tomatoes, then cut both into rough ½-inch chunks. Combine in a bowl.

2. In another bowl, stir together the yogurt, onion, mint, milk, salt, and pepper. Add to the cucumber and tomatoes and stir to combine well. Chill the mixture at least 1 hour or up to 4 hours before serving.

Anise Poached Apricots

Makes 4 servings

Other fruits, such as peaches, nectarines, or plums can also be poached in this syrup. Cooking times will vary slightly according to the size and ripeness of the fruits.

1 pound ripe but firm fresh apricots
⅓ cup honey
½ teaspoon grated lemon zest
1 tablespoon lemon juice
¼ teaspoon anise seed
½ teaspoon vanilla extract

1. Cut the apricots around the circumference through the indentation, twist in half, then discard the pits.

2. In a medium saucepan, combine 3 cups of water with the honey, lemon zest, lemon juice, and anise seed. Bring to a simmer, stirring to dissolve the honey. Add the apricots and simmer, uncovered, over low heat, spooning the syrup over the fruit occasionally, for 8 to 10 minutes, until very tender. Remove the apricots to a bowl with a slotted spoon.

(*continued on next page*)

(*continued*)

3. Bring the syrup to a boil and cook, uncovered, until reduced to about 1½ cups. Remove from the heat and stir in the vanilla. Strain the liquid over the apricots and let cool, then cover and refrigerate for at least 2 hours or up to 24 hours.

4. To serve, spoon the apricots into dessert dishes, adding some of the syrup to each portion.

CHARRED CHICKEN FAJITAS*

SALSA

SLICED AVOCADO AND SHREDDED
LETTUCE GARNISH

BRANDIED PEACH SUNDAES*

Chicken makes wonderful fajitas. The thin coating of oil
protects the meat and allows it to char lightly for a great
smoky flavor. The time-honored way to serve fajitas is to
assemble all the ingredients and allow everyone to build
their own. The sliced avocado and shredded lettuce can be
piled atop the chicken and salsa in the tortilla or it can be
served as a sort of side "salad." Brandied peaches over
vanilla ice cream makes just the right fruity and smoothly
sweet ending for a zesty meal like this.

CHARRED CHICKEN FAJITAS

Makes 4 servings

Chicken thighs have a more robust flavor to hold up to the zesty salsa that accompanies these fajitas—and they tend to be more economical—but breasts can be used, if you prefer.

> **1 pound skinless, boneless chicken thighs**
> **¼ teaspoon salt**
> **⅛ teaspoon black pepper**
> **1½ tablespoons lime juice**
> **1½ tablespoons vegetable oil**
> **4 flour tortillas (7 to 8 inches in diameter)**

1. Use your hands to flatten the chicken thighs to an even thickness of about ½ inch. Season with salt and pepper. In a shallow dish, combine the lime juice and vegetable oil. Add the chicken, turning to coat both sides. Let stand at room temperature for about 20 minutes or refrigerate 1 to 2 hours before cooking.

2. Build a medium-hot barbecue fire. Wrap the tortillas in foil.

3. Grill the chicken, turning once, for 4 to 5 minutes per side, until cooked through and lightly charred on the outside. During the last few minutes of cooking, place the wrapped tortillas at the edge of the grill to warm.

4. To assemble, cut the chicken thinly across the grain. Allow each person to make a fajita by spooning some chicken onto a tortilla, adding salsa, then rolling or folding up the tortilla.

BRANDIED PEACH SUNDAES

Makes 4 servings

Choose really ripe and juicy peaches for this adult sundae.

   4 small or 2 large peaches (about 1 pound total)
   3 tablespoons sugar
   2 teaspoons lemon juice
   3 tablespoons brandy
   1 pint vanilla ice cream or frozen yogurt

1. Peel the peaches by plunging them into a saucepan of boiling water for 10 to 15 seconds, until the skins loosen. Then peel off the skins with your fingers aided by a paring knife.

2. Thinly slice the peaches, then place in a mixing bowl and toss with the sugar, lemon juice, and brandy. Let stand 30 minutes at room temperature or refrigerate about 1 hour to release the juices and dissolve the sugar. Stir again before using.

3. To serve, divide the ice cream among 4 dessert dishes. Spoon the peaches and juices over the ice cream.

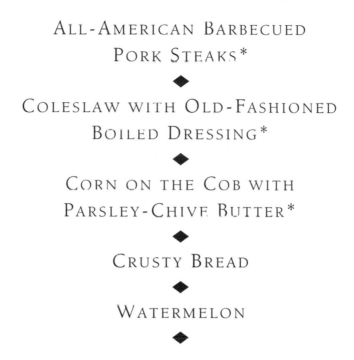

ALL-AMERICAN BARBECUED PORK STEAKS*

◆

COLESLAW WITH OLD-FASHIONED BOILED DRESSING*

◆

CORN ON THE COB WITH PARSLEY-CHIVE BUTTER*

◆

CRUSTY BREAD

◆

WATERMELON

◆

This is heartland cooking at its best. Barbecued pork steaks are a specialty of the Mississippi border towns of southern Illinois, and boiled dressing for coleslaw is popular all over the Midwest. Of course, corn is king there, too. This is a finger-licking meal best eaten outdoors. It is also one that lends itself quite deliciously to doubling and tripling if you are having a party.

ALL-AMERICAN BARBECUED PORK STEAKS

Makes 4 servings

You could use thin-cut pork chops or even boneless chops for this recipe, but it is really more flavorful with the more economical pork steaks cut from the shoulder. These take almost an hour and a quarter to cook—first on the grill and then in the oven—but don't skimp on the time, because the slow cooking and simmering are what makes these "falling-apart" tender.

> **2 pounds pork shoulder steaks, each cut slightly less than ½ inch thick**
> **¼ teaspoon salt**
> **⅛ teaspoon black pepper**
> **2 teaspoons cider vinegar**
> **1 small garlic clove, slivered**
> **2 cups bottled barbecue sauce**

1. Build a medium-hot barbecue fire.

2. Season the pork steaks with the salt and pepper. In a shallow nonaluminum pan, combine 3 cups of water with the vinegar and garlic. Bring to a simmer. Keep warm on the edge of the grill.

3. Grill the pork steaks, turning once, for 1 minute on each side to sear them. Using tongs, dunk the steaks one at a time into the hot vinegar water. Grill on one side for another 3 minutes, then dunk again. Turn the steaks and continue to grill and dunk for a total of about 12 minutes until almost cooked through. Then brush with some of the barbecue sauce and grill about 2 minutes per side.

4. Remove the steaks from the grill and place them in a saucepan or baking dish large enough to hold them comfortably. Pour the remaining barbecue sauce over the grilled meat.

5. Cover and simmer over low heat or bake in a preheated 300 degree oven for 45 minutes to 1 hour, until the meat is very tender and falling off the bone. (If the sauce seems thin, simmer or bake, uncovered, for the last 10 minutes or so.) Spoon off any excess fat that accumulates on the top. (This recipe can be made a day ahead and reheated over low heat or in a microwave.) Serve the meat covered with sauce.

COLESLAW WITH OLD-FASHIONED BOILED DRESSING

Makes 4 very generous servings

This makes a generous amount, but then there is no point in making just a little coleslaw.

1½ tablespoons sugar
1 tablespoon all-purpose flour
1¼ teaspoons dry mustard
¾ teaspoon salt
¼ teaspoon black pepper
¾ cup milk
¼ cup cider vinegar
2 egg yolks
½ teaspoon celery seed
6 cups thinly sliced cabbage (about 1½ pounds)
2 tablespoons minced onion

1. In a heavy saucepan, whisk together the sugar, flour, mustard, salt, and pepper. Slowly whisk in the milk and vinegar until smooth. Cook over medium-high heat for 2

to 3 minutes, stirring constantly, until the mixture thickly coats the back of a spoon and comes to a boil.

2. In a small bowl, lightly beat the yolks, then whisk some of the hot mixture into the yolks to warm them. Scrape the sauce back into the pan, add the celery seed, reduce the heat to medium-low, and cook without boiling, stirring constantly, for 1 or 2 minutes, until the sauce is thickened and smooth.

3. In a mixing bowl, combine the cabbage and onion. Pour the hot dressing over the vegetables and toss to mix thoroughly. Let cool, then refrigerate at least 1 hour or up to 24 hours before serving.

CORN ON THE COB WITH
PARSLEY-CHIVE BUTTER

Makes 4 servings

   3 tablespoons butter
   1 tablespoon minced parsley
   1 tablespoon minced chives
   ¼ teaspoon salt
   ¼ teaspoon black pepper
   4 ears of fresh corn, husked

1. Melt the butter in a small saucepan over low heat. Add the parsley, chives, salt, and pepper. (The herb butter can be made several hours ahead. Remelt to use.)

2. Cook the corn in a large pot of boiling water for 6 to 8 minutes, until tender. Alternatively, place the ears in a single layer in a shallow microwave-safe dish. Add about ¼ cup water. Cover tightly with microwave-safe plastic wrap and microwave on high for 6 to 8 minutes; let stand 2 minutes. Drizzle or brush the corn with the parsley-chive butter.

Summer Vegetable and Tofu Stir-Fry*

◆

Hot and Sour Peanut Noodles*

◆

Rice Crackers

◆

Cantaloupe Drizzled with Fresh Lime Juice

◆

Stir-fry dishes are always quick, once you have all the ingredients ready. This recipe, unlike some that have an innumerable number of painstakingly diced components, is also simple and easy to put together. Without the tofu, it makes a fine vegetable side dish for simply broiled meats or poultry. But with the added tofu, it becomes the main course itself. Teamed with highly spiced noodles, this healthful dish makes an appealing and filling meal. Lime, the prime citrus fruit of summer, adds zest to the peanut sauce and also perks up the fresh cantaloupe for dessert.

SUMMER VEGETABLE AND TOFU STIR-FRY

Makes 4 servings

The cilantro adds a really pleasant dimension to this otherwise lightly seasoned dish, but it is not crucial. Be sure to have all ingredients ready before beginning to stir-fry.

**8 to 10 ounces firm tofu
1 red or yellow bell pepper
6 ounces snow peas
½ bunch of scallions
3 tablespoons vegetable oil
1 tablespoon soy sauce
⅛ teaspoon hot pepper flakes
3 tablespoons chopped cilantro (optional)**

1. Cut the tofu into ¾-inch cubes and dry the cubes on paper towels. Thinly slice the bell pepper. Remove the strings from the snow peas and cut any especially large ones in half diagonally. Thinly slice the scallions, including the green.

2. In a wok or large heavy skillet, heat the oil. Add the tofu and stir-fry over high heat for 1 to 2 minutes, until lightly browned. Add the bell pepper and stir-fry 30 seconds. Add the snow peas and stir-fry for 30 seconds. Add the scallions and stir-fry for 30 seconds. Add the soy sauce and hot pepper and stir-fry for about 30 seconds. Stir in the cilantro and serve at once.

HOT AND SOUR PEANUT NOODLES

Makes 4 servings

Readily available conventional dried vermicelli is about the same size as Oriental soba noodles. Use either one.

⅔ **cup chunky peanut butter**
3 **garlic cloves, minced**
¼ **teaspoon grated lime zest**
⅓ **cup fresh lime juice**
2 **tablespoons soy sauce**
½ **teaspoon hot pepper flakes**
1 **cup chicken broth**
10 **ounces vermicelli pasta or Oriental soba noodles**

(*continued on next page*)

(*continued*)

1. In a food processor or by hand with a whisk, mix together the peanut butter, garlic, lime zest, lime juice, soy sauce, and hot pepper until well blended. Process or whisk in the broth until smooth. (The peanut sauce can be made about 2 hours ahead.)

2. Cook the pasta in boiling salted water until *al dente,* tender but firm, for about 6 minutes for vermicelli or about 3 minutes for Oriental noodles. Drain well.

3. Add the peanut sauce to the hot noodles and toss gently to coat the pasta with sauce.

PIZZA BURGERS*

◆

GARLIC GRILLED ITALIAN BREADS*

◆

MARINATED GREEN BEANS*

◆

RASPBERRY ICE

◆

These burgers, with their summery garnishes and accompanying toasted breads, have all the components of a perfect picnic—Italian style. The green beans, marinated in lemon vinaigrette, add an even more sprightly touch to this colorful meal. Raspberry ice or sherbet is a light and simple ending to a menu full of robust flavors.

Pizza Burgers

Makes 4 servings

 1½ pounds ground chuck
 2 teaspoons chopped fresh basil or ½ teaspoon dried
 4 slices of mozzarella cheese
 Salt and black pepper
 4 slices of sweet onion
 4 slices of ripe tomato
 8 large fresh basil leaves

1. Build a medium-hot barbecue fire.

2. Lightly mix the meat with the chopped basil. Divide into 4 portions and shape into patties about 4 inches in diameter. Grill the meat, turning once, for 5 to 8 minutes per side, until charred on the outside and the desired degree of doneness on the inside. About 2 minutes before the burgers are done, top with the cheese slices to melt. Season with salt and pepper.

3. Serve each burger topped with an onion and tomato slice and 2 basil leaves.

Garlic Grilled Italian Breads

Makes 4 servings

Sandwich Pizza Burgers with these grilled breads or serve them alongside. If you are not using the grill for dinner, these can be broiled indoors.

   ¼ **cup olive oil**
   1 tablespoon balsamic vinegar
   1 garlic clove, crushed through a press
   ¼ **teaspoon hot pepper flakes**
   ⅛ **teaspoon salt**
   8 slices of Italian bread, cut between ¼ inch and
      ½ **inch thick**

1. Build a medium-hot barbecue fire.

2. In a small bowl, whisk together the olive oil, vinegar, garlic, hot pepper, and salt.

3. Grill the bread about 30 seconds per side until lightly toasted. Liberally brush one side of the toasted breads with the garlic-oil mixture and serve warm.

MARINATED GREEN BEANS

Makes 4 servings

 ½ pound green beans
 2 tablespoons lemon juice
 ¼ teaspoon grated lemon zest
 ½ teaspoon Dijon mustard
 ⅛ teaspoon salt
 ⅛ teaspoon black pepper
 2 tablespoons olive oil
 2 tablespoons vegetable oil

1. Trim the beans, but leave whole. Cook in a large saucepan of boiling salted water for about 3 minutes, until crisp-tender. Drain into a colander, then rinse under cold running water to set the color and stop the cooking process. (The beans can be cooked up to 4 hours ahead and refrigerated.)

2. In a small bowl, combine the lemon juice, lemon zest, mustard, salt, and pepper. Stir or whisk in the olive oil and vegetable oil until blended.

3. Toss the vinaigrette with the beans to coat them thoroughly. Refrigerate at least 1 hour or up to 4 hours before serving.

Jack Cheese, Tomato, and Hot Pepper Pasta*

Green Salad

Mocha Wafers*

Sliced Nectarines

This menu has a distinctly Southwest American slant, but with some variations on the theme. The pasta dish is really a warm salad. The residual heat of the cooking pot and the hot pasta act to barely melt the cheese as it brings out the full flavor of the good, ripe tomatoes. A green salad rounds out the meal nicely. Sweet, juicy nectarines make a lovely contrast to thin, dark chocolate cookies.

JACK CHEESE, TOMATO, AND HOT PEPPER PASTA

Makes 4 servings

1½ pounds fresh plum tomatoes
½ cup olive oil
2 tablespoons red wine vinegar
1 teaspoon salt
2 garlic cloves, minced
1 or 2 fresh or canned jalapeño peppers, seeded and
    minced
6 ounces Monterey Jack cheese, finely diced
1 pound penne or ziti
¼ cup chopped cilantro or 1 tablespoon dried
    cilantro plus 3 tablespoons chopped parsley

1. Core, seed, and coarsely chop the tomatoes. In a mixing bowl, combine the tomatoes with the oil, vinegar, salt, garlic, jalapeños, and cheese. (The sauce can be prepared 2 hours ahead.)

2. Cook the pasta in a large pot of boiling salted water for about 10 minutes, until *al dente,* tender but firm. Drain well in a colander.

3. Pour the sauce into the bottom of the still-warm pasta cooking pot, add the cilantro, then return the pasta to the pot. Toss, allowing the residual heat of the pasta and the pot to warm the sauce and begin to melt the cheese.

MOCHA WAFERS

Makes about 40 cookies

The usual cylindrical refrigerator cookie roll is shaped here into a rectangle to make square wafers. The dough freezes well; and you will have a second log that can be baked for a sweet ending to another meal.

   1 ounce unsweetened chocolate, chopped
   1 cup all-purpose flour
   ½ teaspoon baking powder
   ¼ teaspoon baking soda
   ⅛ teaspoon salt
   6 tablespoons (¾ stick) butter, softened
   ⅓ cup plus 3 tablespoons granulated sugar
   ¼ cup packed light brown sugar
   1½ teaspoons instant coffee powder
   1 egg yolk
   1 teaspoon vanilla extract

(continued on next page)

(*continued*)

1. Melt the chocolate in a small bowl set over hot water or in a microwave oven. Sift or whisk together the flour, baking powder, baking soda, and salt.

2. In a mixer bowl, cream together the butter, ⅓ cup of the granulated sugar, and the brown sugar until light and fluffy. Beat in the coffee powder, egg yolk, and vanilla until well blended. With the mixer on low speed, blend in the flour.

3. Form the dough into 2 rolls about 1 inch in diameter. Wrap in plastic wrap, and use your hands to form each roll into a rectangle with 4 fairly even sides. Refrigerate at least 3 hours or up to 3 days. During the first hour of chilling, use your hands and a countertop to reinforce and firm up the 4-sided rectangular shape of the dough.

4. Preheat the oven to 375 degrees. Using a sharp knife, slice the dough ⅛ inch thick. Place the cookies 1 inch apart on ungreased baking sheets. Sprinkle the tops of the cookies lightly with the remaining 3 tablespoons granulated sugar.

5. Bake for 7 to 9 minutes, until set but not browned on the edges. Do not overbake. Transfer the cookies to racks to cool completely. (Store in an airtight container for up to 3 days or freeze for up to 2 months.)

COLD COOKED CHICKEN OR TURKEY

♦

SKILLET RATATOUILLE*

♦

BASIL CORNBREAD*

♦

CHERRIES WITH VANILLA
CUSTARD SAUCE*

♦

This is the perfect meal for times when you have a bit of
leftover cooked poultry or even meat, though the
ratatouille and cornbread are hearty enough to stand
together as a meatless main course by themselves. As in
most stews, the exact quantity of the vegetables is not
particularly important, it is the quality of the summer
produce that makes the difference here. For the cornbread,
a choice of oil or butter is given. The vanilla custard sauce
is also delicious on other seasonal fruits, such as peaches,
nectarines, or blueberries. It can also turn a plain brownie
into an elegant dessert.

SKILLET RATATOUILLE

Makes 4 servings

¼ cup olive oil
1 large onion, thinly sliced
3 large garlic cloves, minced
1 small eggplant, cut into ¾-inch cubes
1 small zucchini, sliced
1 small yellow crookneck squash, sliced
1 green bell pepper, sliced
¾ teaspoon dried marjoram or 1 tablespoon chopped fresh
½ teaspoon dried thyme or 2 teaspoons chopped fresh
½ teaspoon salt
½ teaspoon black pepper
1 pound fresh plum tomatoes
1 tablespoon capers (optional)

1. Heat the olive oil in a large nonaluminum skillet with a lid. Add the onion and cook for 4 minutes over medium-low heat, then add the garlic and cook 1 minute longer, until the vegetables are just softened.

2. Add the eggplant, zucchini, crookneck squash, and bell pepper to the skillet and cook, stirring, for 2 minutes. Season with the marjoram, thyme, salt, and pepper. Cover the pan and simmer over low heat for 20 minutes.

3. Meanwhile, core the tomatoes and cut each into 6 wedges. Add the tomatoes to the skillet, cover, and simmer 8 minutes, or until tomatoes are softened. Stir in the capers, then simmer, uncovered, about 2 minutes, until the liquid is lightly reduced. (This recipe can be made a day ahead and reheated gently.)

BASIL CORNBREAD

Makes 12 to 16 squares

These can also be baked as twelve separate corn muffins. If you do this, bake for about 15 minutes in a 425 degree oven until golden.

1 cup yellow cornmeal
1 cup all-purpose flour
2 tablespoons sugar
4 teaspoons baking powder
¾ teaspoon salt
¼ teaspoon black pepper
1 egg
1 cup milk
¼ cup vegetable oil or melted butter or a
    combination
3 tablespoons chopped fresh basil or 1 tablespoon
    dried

1. Preheat the oven to 425 degrees. Lightly grease an 8- or 9-inch square baking pan.

2. In a large bowl, whisk together the cornmeal, flour, sugar, baking powder, salt, and pepper. In a smaller bowl,

whisk together the egg, milk, oil, and basil until well blended. Make a well in the center of the dry ingredients and pour the liquids in all at once. Stir with a spoon just until all of the flour is moistened. Do not overmix. Spread the batter in the prepared pan, using the spoon to smooth the top.

3. Bake for 18 to 22 minutes, until the top is light golden and a cake tester inserted in the center comes out clean. Serve warm.

CHERRIES WITH VANILLA CUSTARD SAUCE

Makes 4 servings

> 1½ cups half-and-half or light cream
> 4 egg yolks
> ⅓ cup sugar
> 1¼ teaspoons vanilla extract
> 2 cups pitted fresh or thawed frozen dark sweet
>   cherries, such as Bing cherries

1. In a heavy saucepan, bring the half-and-half just to a simmer. Meanwhile, whisk the egg yolks with the sugar in a small bowl until light in color. Slowly whisk the hot cream into the yolk mixture to warm it, then return it to the saucepan. Cook over low heat, stirring almost constantly, for about 10 minutes, until the custard is thick enough to coat the back of a spoon heavily. Do not allow to boil.

2. Pour the custard into a shallow bowl, let cool for about 5 minutes, then stir in the vanilla. Cover and refrigerate for at least 1 hour or up to 24 hours before using.

3. To serve the dessert, spoon the custard sauce into the bottom of 4 shallow dessert bowls. Top with the cherries.

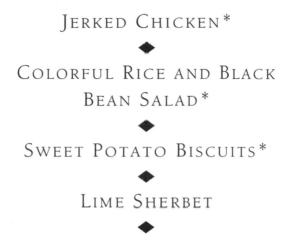

Jerked Chicken*

◆

Colorful Rice and Black Bean Salad*

◆

Sweet Potato Biscuits*

◆

Lime Sherbet

◆

Caribbean food is "hot stuff," both in terms of spiciness and culinary fashion. It's no wonder people are taking to these dishes, since they are colorful, full of flavor, and emphasize the vegetables, fruits, and starches that are the foundations of a healthy, economical diet. There are as many variations of jerked chicken, a Jamaican barbecue specialty, as there are good cooks on the island. Instead of grilling the chicken as recommended here, it can be baked in a 375 degree oven for 35 to 45 minutes. Rice and beans, a staple combination throughout the region, are used here to make a bright salad to accompany the spicy chicken. Sweet potato biscuits are a combination of all-American cooking and Caribbean ingredients. Lime sherbet provides the perfect refreshing ending for this meal.

JERKED CHICKEN

Makes 4 servings

⅓ cup vegetable oil
3 tablespoons white wine vinegar
1½ tablespoons lime juice
1 tablespoon sugar
¼ cup minced scallions, including green tops
2 garlic cloves, minced
1 jalapeño pepper, fresh or canned, seeded and
    minced
1 teaspoon dried thyme
½ teaspoon ground allspice
½ teaspoon ground cinnamon
½ teaspoon salt
½ teaspoon black pepper
¼ to ½ teaspoon cayenne, to taste
3 pounds cut-up chicken parts

1. Combine the oil, vinegar, lime juice, sugar, scallions, garlic, jalapeño pepper, thyme, allspice, cinnamon, salt, black pepper, and cayenne in a shallow nonaluminum dish large enough to hold the chicken in a single layer. Whisk to dissolve the sugar.

2. Place the chicken in the dish, turn to coat, and use your fingers to rub some of the marinade beneath the skin. Let stand 20 minutes at room temperature or refrigerate for up to 24 hours. Meanwhile, build a medium-hot barbecue fire.

3. Grill the chicken, turning, for 20 to 25 minutes, until lightly charred on the outside, no longer pink near the bone.

COLORFUL RICE AND BLACK BEAN SALAD

Makes 4 servings

You can cook your own dried black beans or use drained beans from a 14- or 16-ounce can. Two-thirds cup raw rice can be cooked fresh for the salad, but this is also an ideal way to use up leftover rice.

VINAIGRETTE
3 tablespoons white wine vinegar
2 teaspoons Dijon mustard, preferably coarse grain
1 teaspoon ground cumin
½ teaspoon salt
¼ teaspoon black pepper
½ cup olive oil
¼ to ½ teaspoon hot pepper sauce

SALAD

2 cups cooked long-grain rice
1½ cups cooked black beans
1 cup (about 8 ounces) seeded and diced plum
** tomatoes**
1 green bell pepper, cut in rough ¼-inch dice
½ cup coarsely chopped red onion
8 leaves of Boston or red leaf lettuce

1. To make the vinaigrette, combine the vinegar, mustard, cumin, salt, and pepper in a small bowl. Stir or whisk in the olive oil, then whisk in the hot sauce to taste.

2. For the salad, combine the rice, beans, tomatoes, bell pepper, and onion in a large bowl. Add the vinaigrette and toss to mix well. Let stand about 30 minutes at room temperature or up to 3 hours in the refrigerator before serving.

3. To serve, arrange the lettuce leaves on a platter or on individual plates. Spoon the salad onto the lettuce.

SWEET POTATO BISCUITS

Makes about 12 biscuits

Sweet potato adds color, moistness, and a subtle flavor to these biscuits. Don't use canned sweet potatoes, because they are almost always packed in a very sweet syrup. Fresh sweet potatoes are inexpensive and fast to cook in a microwave oven.

   1 small sweet potato (about 6 ounces)
   3 tablespoons milk
   1 cup all-purpose flour
   1½ teaspoons baking powder
   1½ teaspoons sugar
   ½ teaspoon salt
   2 tablespoons chilled butter, cut into small pieces
   1 tablespoon chilled solid vegetable shortening, cut
      into small pieces

1. Prick the sweet potato, then cook in a microwave oven on High for 4 to 5 minutes; or bake, wrapped in foil, in a conventional oven at 375 degrees for about 1 hour, until the potato is very tender. Let cool, then peel and mash with

a fork to make ½ cup. Reserve any extra for another use or eat it on the spot. Blend the milk into the mashed sweet potato and set aside. (The recipe can be prepared to this point up to a day ahead and refrigerated. Let return to room temperature before continuing.)

2. Preheat the oven to 425 degrees. Lightly grease a baking sheet.

3. In a medium mixing bowl, sift or whisk together the flour, baking powder, sugar, and salt. Cut the butter and shortening into the flour until the mixture resembles small peas. Using a fork, gently beat in the mashed sweet potato to make a soft but manageable dough.

4. Turn the dough onto a lightly floured surface and knead 3 times. Roll or pat to ½ inch thick. Cut into rounds with a 2-inch biscuit cutter. Reroll and cut the scraps.

5. Place the biscuits 2 inches apart on the prepared baking sheet. Bake for 14 to 17 minutes, until golden brown and well risen. Serve warm. (Leftovers can be frozen, then reheated for a few minutes in a 350 degree oven.)

CORN AND CHEESE CHOWDER*

PILOT CRACKERS

CHERRY TOMATO AND
WATERCRESS SALAD*

POUND CAKE WITH DOUBLE
BLUEBERRY SAUCE*

Though most of us think of chowder as a soup with potatoes, clams, and milk, the name really stems from the *"chaudière"*—the pot in which the soup is cooked. This is a purely vegetable chowder, especially well suited to an unexpected cool summer day. Pilot crackers are the classic New England accompaniment to chowder, but any plain crisp cracker will do just as well. The salad can be served as a first course or on a separate plate along with the chowder. Toasting pound cake really enhances its flavor, especially for the store-bought version. The sauce is also excellent as is on angel food cake or warmed slightly and ladled over vanilla ice cream.

CORN AND CHEESE CHOWDER

Makes 4 servings

3 tablespoons butter
1 large onion, chopped
1 cup chopped celery
1 tablespoon flour
2 teaspoons dry mustard
¼ teaspoon cayenne
2 cups chicken broth
2 cups peeled and diced potatoes (about 12 ounces)
1 teaspoon dried thyme
3 cups corn kernels, fresh or frozen
3 cups half-and-half
2 cups shredded Cheddar cheese (8 ounces)
Salt
½ cup thinly sliced scallions

1. In a large heavy saucepan, melt the butter over medium-low heat. Add the onion and celery and cook for about 4 minutes, until the vegetables are just softened. Add the

flour, mustard, and cayenne and cook, stirring, for 2 minutes. Stir in the broth and bring to a simmer. Add the potatoes and thyme. Lower the heat, cover, and simmer for 10 minutes, until the potatoes are nearly fork-tender. Add the corn and half-and-half. Simmer, covered, for 5 minutes, until the vegetables are tender.

2. With the pan set half off the heat, add the cheese by handfuls, stirring until each addition is melted before adding another. Taste and add salt and additional cayenne if needed. Serve garnished with the scallions.

CHERRY TOMATO AND
WATERCRESS SALAD

Makes 4 servings

2 tablespoons red wine vinegar
1 small garlic clove, minced
½ teaspoon Dijon mustard
¼ teaspoon salt
⅛ teaspoon black pepper
¼ cup olive oil
2 tablespoons vegetable oil
1 large or 2 small bunches of watercress
16 small cherry tomatoes

1. To make the vinaigrette, combine the vinegar, garlic, mustard, salt, and pepper in a small bowl. Whisk in the olive oil and vegetable oil.

2. For the salad, trim any thick stems from the watercress. Rinse and dry well. In a large bowl, toss the watercress with the vinaigrette to coat the leaves. Arrange the watercress on 4 individual salad plates. Top with the tomatoes.

POUND CAKE WITH DOUBLE BLUEBERRY SAUCE

Makes 4 servings

  2 cups fresh or frozen blueberries
  ¼ cup sugar
  ⅛ teaspoon ground mace
  1½ teaspoons lemon juice
  ¼ teaspoon vanilla extract
  4 slices of pound cake—purchased or homemade

1. In a medium nonaluminum saucepan, bring half of the blueberries, the sugar, mace, and the lemon juice to a simmer over medium heat, stirring constantly to dissolve the sugar and release the juices in the berries. Simmer gently for 3 minutes, stirring constantly. Add the remaining berries and simmer for 1 minute. Remove from the heat. Stir in the vanilla. (The blueberry sauce can be made a day ahead. Refrigerate, but serve at room temperature.)

2. To serve, lightly toast both sides of the pound cake under a broiler. Ladle the room-temperature blueberry sauce over the warm slices.

Autumn

◆

Autumn is the season of harvest, on the farm and in the kitchen. It is a time of so much abundance that a cook's culinary imagination can run riot, no matter how large or small the budget may be. It is now that apples are hawked along roadsides in bushel baskets. Even supermarkets display a variety and quality that demonstrate empirically why the apple has become the quintessential American fruit. There is also a profusion of late tomatoes—some still green—eggplants and peppers. As fall wears on, pears and prune plums have their day in the sun, as do sweet potatoes and all sorts of cool-weather squashes. These vegetables are good keepers, and they'll remain an excellent value well into the winter months.

Pork and chicken are often featured as weekly specials. Many of the chicken recipes throughout this book simply call for "cut-up chicken" or "chicken parts." The idea is to use whichever cut is the best buy of the week. As the season progresses, look for turkey to be at its lowest price of the year. An interest in baking returns, which spurs markets to offer staples, such as flour, sugar, nuts, and chocolate chips at below regular cost. Now is the time to stock up the pantry.

CAPELLINI WITH HERBED WHITE CLAM SAUCE*

◆

THIN BREAD STICKS

◆

ROASTED PEPPER AND CURLY ENDIVE SALAD*

◆

LEMON SHERBET WITH CANDIED LEMON SYRUP*

◆

This menu is sure to become an instant favorite because it is full of enticing flavors. The pasta sauce is brimming with garlic, oregano, and basil—a trio that has become an American kitchen standard. Clams have a natural affinity for these flavors and make a seafood dish that everyone loves. Home-roasted red bell peppers give a rich, smoky taste that no raw pepper can ever attain. Finally, a sweet/tart lemon zest syrup spiked with rum turns plain lemon sherbet into a dessert for guests. In fact, this whole meal, though easily prepared, is eminently worthy of a special occasion for family and/or friends.

Capellini with Herbed White Clam Sauce

Makes 4 servings

Other thin strand pasta can be used here. Inexpensive and convenient, chopped fresh clams are available in many seafood markets.

3 tablespoons butter
⅓ cup olive oil
3 garlic cloves, minced
1½ cups clam juice (see Note)
⅓ cup dry white wine
1 teaspoon dried oregano
½ teaspoon dried basil
⅛ teaspoon hot pepper flakes
1 pound capellini
2 cups drained chopped fresh clams or three 7-ounce
    cans chopped clams, juices reserved (see Note)
⅓ cup chopped parsley
Salt and black pepper

(*continued on next page*)

(*continued*)

1. In a large skillet, melt the butter in the olive oil over medium-low heat. Add the garlic and cook for 1 minute. Add the clam juice, wine, oregano, basil, and hot pepper. Simmer, uncovered, for 5 to 7 minutes, until reduced by about one-fourth. (This recipe can be prepared to this point about 2 hours ahead; reserve at room temperature.)

2. Cook the capellini in a large pot of boiling salted water for 5 to 7 minutes, until *al dente,* tender but firm. Drain well.

3. If necessary, return the sauce to a simmer. Add the chopped clams and all but 1 tablespoon of the parsley. Simmer for 1 minute until heated through. Taste and add salt and pepper if needed. (No salt will probably be needed since clam juice is quite salty.)

4. Toss the sauce with the hot pasta. Sprinkle the remaining 1 tablespoon parsley on top.

NOTE: Use drained juices from the clams plus enough bottled clam juice to make up the quantity needed.

Roasted Pepper and
Curly Endive Salad

Makes 4 servings

In early autumn, red bell peppers are usually plentiful and well priced. At other times of the year, when they can be costly, jarred roasted peppers are a fine alternative.

3 tablespoons balsamic vinegar
2 teaspoons minced shallot
¼ teaspoon salt
⅛ teaspoon black pepper
¼ cup plus 2 tablespoons olive oil
1 large red bell pepper
1 small head of curly endive or escarole

1. To make the vinaigrette, whisk together the vinegar, shallot, salt, and pepper in a small bowl. Slowly whisk in the olive oil until blended.

2. To roast the pepper, preheat the broiler. Place the pepper on a large piece of aluminum foil. Set under the broiler, about 3 inches from the heat source. Roast the pepper, turning until the skin of the whole pepper is charred, about

5 minutes. Wrap the pepper completely in the aluminum foil and let cool for a few minutes until it can be handled. Then use your fingers and a small, sharp knife to peel off the skin. Cut the pepper into strips about 1½ inches by ½ inch, discarding the seeds.

3. Place the pepper strips in a small bowl and pour 2 tablespoons of the vinaigrette over them. Let stand at room temperature for about 15 minutes, or refrigerate for up to 4 hours.

4. Trim the tough ribs from the curly endive and rinse the leaves well because they are often gritty. Dry the endive, then tear it into bite-sized pieces. In a salad bowl, toss the endive with the remaining vinaigrette, then add the pepper strips and any liquid. Toss again.

LEMON SHERBET WITH CANDIED LEMON SYRUP

Makes 4 servings

Smaller lemons that yield a bit to pressure have more juice and are thus a better buy than bigger ones that are thick skinned and rock hard.

2 small lemons
¼ cup sugar
1 tablespoon rum
1 pint lemon sherbet

1. Use a small, sharp knife or zesting tool to peel thin slices of lemon zest, each between ½ and ¾ inch long. Squeeze 1 tablespoon juice from the lemons and reserve.

2. Place the zest in a small saucepan and cover with about 1 inch of water. Bring to a boil, then lower the heat, cover, and simmer for 5 minutes. Drain the zest into a small strainer and thoroughly rinse under cold running water.

3. In a small saucepan, stir together the sugar and 3 tablespoons water. Bring to a boil, stirring to dissolve the sugar. Cover the pan for 30 seconds to wash down any undissolved sugar crystals. Uncover, add the lemon zest, and simmer for 2 minutes. Remove from the heat, then stir in the reserved lemon juice and the rum. Let cool completely before using. (The syrup can be made 2 days ahead and refrigerated.)

4. To serve, scoop the sherbet into 4 dessert bowls or goblets. Spoon the lemon syrup and zest over each serving.

CORIANDER-GINGER CARROT SOUP*

◆

ROAST BEEF AND BROCCOLI SALAD*

◆

HERBED PITA TOASTS*

◆

GREEN AND RED GRAPES

◆

This contemporary American menu, perfect for a football season tailgate feast, has Oriental overtones in the seasonings. A brilliant carrot puree serves as the base for a light yet creamy soup. Ground coriander and ginger give it a delicate and slightly exotic flavor sensation. The punch of garlic and soy sauce make the simple main-course roast beef and broccoli composed salad very special. Crisp, cumin-scented pita wedges are a fine accompaniment to both soup and salad.

If you wish to transport the meal to a picnic site, take the soup in a Thermos, pack the salad components separately and assemble upon arrival; carry the pita toasts in a plastic bag. The grapes can also be bagged, then set out in a bowl or on a tray when needed.

Coriander-Ginger Carrot Soup

Makes 4 servings

¼ cup vegetable oil
1 large onion, chopped
1½ pounds carrots, chopped
½ teaspoon ground ginger
¼ teaspoon ground coriander
2 cups chicken broth
1½ cups half-and-half or light cream
3 tablespoons chopped parsley
½ teaspoon salt
⅛ teaspoon pepper

1. In a large heavy saucepan, heat the oil. Add the onion and carrots, cover, and cook over low heat for 5 minutes, stirring once or twice. Add the ginger, coriander, chicken broth, and about ½ cup of water, or enough so that the liquid just covers the vegetables. Simmer, covered, over low heat for 30 minutes, or until the carrots are very tender.

2. Puree the soup in a food processor; return to the pan. Add the half-and-half, 2 cups water, and 2 tablespoons parsley. Reheat but do not boil. Season with salt and pepper. Serve hot or cold, garnished with the remaining parsley.

ROAST BEEF AND BROCCOLI SALAD

Makes 4 servings

You could use leftover steak or roast beef here, or else buy it from the deli. Thinly sliced meat seems to taste better and go further, too.

GARLIC-SOY VINAIGRETTE
3 tablespoons red wine vinegar
1 tablespoon soy sauce
½ teaspoon black pepper
2 garlic cloves, minced
¼ cup olive oil
¼ cup vegetable oil

SALAD
1 bunch of broccoli (about 1 pound)
1 small head of red leaf or romaine lettuce,
separated into leaves
½ pound medium-rare roast beef, thinly sliced
¼ pound mushrooms, thinly sliced

1. To make the vinaigrette, combine the vinegar, soy sauce, pepper, and garlic in a small bowl. Blend well. Slowly whisk in the olive oil and vegetable oil until blended.

2. For the salad, trim the broccoli into spears, then cook in a large saucepan of boiling salted water for 4 to 5 minutes, until crisp-tender. Drain in a colander, then rinse under cold running water to stop the cooking and set the color. (The broccoli can be cooked several hours ahead. Set aside at room temperature.)

3. To assemble the salad, line a large platter or individual plates with the lettuce leaves. Arrange the roast beef, slices rolled up if they are thin enough, in the center of the platter. Toss the mushrooms with about 2 tablespoons of the dressing, then spoon them to one side of the meat. Toss the broccoli with about 3 tablespoons of the dressing and arrange the spears on the other side of the meat. Drizzle the remaining dressing over the entire salad.

HERBED PITA TOASTS

Makes 4 servings

   2 pita breads
   1 tablespoon plus 2 teaspoons olive oil
   ¼ teaspoon ground cumin
   ¼ teaspoon salt
   ⅛ teaspoon black pepper
   1½ tablespoons minced parsley

1. Preheat the broiler. Split the pita breads by carefully running a small knife around the edges and then lifting the two halves apart.

2. In a small bowl, stir together the olive oil, cumin, salt, and pepper. Brush the cut sides of the pita breads with the seasoned oil. Sprinkle the parsley over the breads.

3. Broil about 4 inches from the heat source for about 1 minute, until the bread is golden brown and crisp. Cut or break each toast into rough quarters.

BACON AND CHEDDAR CHICKEN*

◆

BAKED CONFETTI RICE*

◆

BRAISED GREEN PEAS

◆

PURPLE PLUM AND OATMEAL CRISP*

◆

This is a wonderful supper for an early autumn evening when you want to get back into the kitchen after a summer of barbecuing and main-course salads. The chicken is cooked in minutes while the rice bakes in the oven. Stir in the tomatoes last so that they keep their texture and bright color. Good-quality frozen peas are one of those vegetables that are often better than fresh (and are certainly cheaper and a lot less work). If all else fails to bring you indoors, the aroma of the plum crisp baking will certainly do it. By the way, you can bake both the rice and the dessert at the same time, if you wish.

BACON AND CHEDDAR CHICKEN

Makes 4 servings

You can buy already shredded Cheddar cheese, but it is almost always more expensive than doing it yourself, and the flavor can be very bland. Chicken cutlets are usually thinly sliced. If the ones your market carries are not, use your hand to flatten them to slightly less than ½ inch in thickeness.

4 slices of bacon
½ cup unseasoned dry bread crumbs
½ teaspoon dried thyme
¼ teaspoon dried savory
¼ teaspoon salt
¼ teaspoon black pepper
1 egg
1 pound skinless, boneless chicken thighs or breast cutlets
1 cup shredded Cheddar cheese (4 ounces)

1. In a large skillet, fry the bacon until crisp. Drain on paper towels, crumble, and reserve for garnish. Discard all but 3 tablespoons drippings from the skillet.

2. In a shallow dish, combine the bread crumbs, thyme, savory, salt, and pepper. In another shallow dish, lightly beat the egg.

3. Dip the chicken first into the egg, then into the crumbs to coat. (The recipe can be prepared to this point up to 3 hours ahead. Refrigerate the cutlets in a single layer.)

4. Sauté the chicken cutlets in the bacon drippings over medium-high heat, turning once, for 2 to 3 minutes per side, until the coating is golden brown and the chicken is cooked through. About 1 minute before the chicken is done, top with the cheese and bacon, then cover the skillet so the cheese will melt and the bacon will heat.

BAKED CONFETTI RICE

Makes 4 servings

Baking is a simple, flexible way to cook rice since it needs little attention, and it will hold for up to 30 minutes in a turned-off oven.

   1½ tablespoons olive oil or butter
   1 carrot, chopped
   1 medium onion, chopped
   1 garlic clove
   ¾ cup long-grain white rice
   1½ cups boiling water or chicken broth
   ¼ teaspoon salt
   ¼ teaspoon black pepper
   ⅓ cup seeded and diced fresh plum tomatoes

1. Preheat the oven to 375 degrees. In a medium saucepan, heat the oil or butter. Add the carrot and onion and cook over medium-low heat for 4 minutes, until nearly softened. Add the garlic and cook 1 minute. Add the rice and toss to coat all the grains with oil. Turn into a 1- or 1½-quart baking dish or casserole. Pour the boiling water or broth over the rice and season with the salt and pepper. Stir to combine.

2. Cover the casserole and bake 30 minutes, or until the rice is tender and all of the liquid is absorbed.

3. Before serving, use a fork to mix in the tomatoes and fluff the rice.

Purple Plum and Oatmeal Crisp

Makes 4 servings

This is best served warm, soon after baking, when the topping is most crisp. But refrigerated leftovers make a great breakfast, too.

6 tablespoons butter
1½ pounds pitted and quartered prune plums (about 4 cups)
1 tablespoon orange juice
⅔ cup sugar
½ cup all-purpose flour
⅓ cup old-fashioned or quick-cooking oats
¾ teaspoon ground cinnamon

1. Preheat the oven to 375 degrees. Use about 1 teaspoon of the butter to grease a 9-inch pie dish.

2. Toss the plums with the orange juice and ⅓ cup of the sugar. Spread in the buttered pie dish.

3. In a food processor, combine the remaining ⅓ cup sugar, the flour, oats, and cinnamon. Pulse to blend. Cut the remaining butter into 10 pieces and distribute over the dry ingredients. Pulse about 10 times until crumbly. (The topping can also be mixed by hand in a bowl; rub the butter in with your fingers.) Sprinkle the topping over the plums.

4. Bake for 45 minutes, or until the plums are tender and the topping is crisp and browned.

NOTE: Prune plums are best suited to baking; many other varieties are too watery. If you can't find them, use another rather firm purple plum, slice them about ½ inch thick, and add 1 tablespoon flour when you toss the plums with the sugar.

CAJUN FRIED CATFISH ON A SESAME BUN*

◆

TARTAR SAUCE OR MAYONNAISE

◆

SWEET AND SOUR COLESLAW*

◆

MINT CHOCOLATE CHIP ICE CREAM

◆

Sandwich suppers are welcomed by everyone, especially after a busy day. This informal menu highlights the new, but now readily available farm-raised catfish. These firm, white-fleshed fish fillets are consistently mild and sweet in flavor. An added bonus is that they are also one of the best buys in the fish market. Served up on a sesame bun, this pan-fried fish sandwich is contemporary, especially when accompanied by a light, sweet and sour coleslaw. Finish off this meal with a splurge of mint chocolate chip ice cream.

Cajun Fried Catfish on a Sesame Bun

Makes 4 servings

> 3 tablespoons all-purpose flour
> 3 tablespoons yellow cornmeal
> ½ teaspoon salt
> ¼ teaspoon cayenne
> ¼ teaspoon black pepper
> 1 pound catfish or other firm fish fillets
> 3 tablespoons vegetable oil
> 4 sesame sandwich buns
> Tartar sauce or mayonnaise

1. On a large plate, combine the flour, cornmeal, salt, cayenne, and black pepper. Mix well. Dredge the fish in the seasoned flour to coat both sides. Shake off any excess.

2. Heat the oil in a large skillet. Add the fish and cook over medium-high heat, turning carefully with a wide spatula, for 2 to 3 minutes per side, until crusty brown on the outside and just cooked through.

3. Lightly toast the sesame buns and spread the cut sides with tartar sauce, then sandwich with the fried fish.

Sweet and Sour Coleslaw

Makes 4 servings

1 small head of green cabbage (about 1 pound)
1 small green bell pepper
1 medium carrot
1 small onion
3 tablespoons cider or white wine vinegar
1½ tablespoons sugar
1½ teaspoons Dijon mustard
½ teaspoon salt
⅛ teaspoon black pepper
⅓ cup vegetable oil

1. Using a food processor or a sharp knife, thinly slice the cabbage and the bell pepper. Place in a mixing bowl. Using the shredding disc or the coarse side of a grater, shred the carrot and onion. Add to the cabbage and pepper.

2. In a small bowl, whisk together the vinegar, sugar, mustard, salt, and pepper. Slowly whisk in the oil.

3. Pour the dressing over the cabbage mixture and toss until well mixed. Cover and refrigerate at least 1 hour or up to 24 hours before serving, tossing occasionally.

BRAISED CIDER APPLE
PORK CHOPS*

◆

BAKED POTATOES

◆

GARLIC-STEAMED SWISS CHARD*

◆

DEVIL'S FOOD CUPCAKES WITH
CHOCOLATE SATIN ICING*

◆

This menu takes its inspiration from the best of old-fashioned American heartland home cooking. But each dish has a special touch to update it with heightened flavor to create a meal as appropriate for guests as it is for family. The main course makes fine use of today's leaner pork and the splash of vinegar brings out the full flavor of seasonal apples. Garlic gives a pleasant punch to Swiss chard—an underused but very delicious and most nutritious green vegetable. These devil's food cupcakes may be the moistest, darkest, most chocolatey you've ever tasted, and the satiny smooth, slightly tangy chocolate-sour cream icing lifts them far out of the "kid's lunch" category.

Braised Cider Apple Pork Chops

Makes 4 servings

> **4 pork chops, cut ¾ inch thick (1½ to 2 pounds)**
> **Salt and black pepper**
> **2 tablespoons vegetable oil**
> **1 tart apple, peeled, cored, and thinly sliced**
> **1 large onion, thinly sliced**
> **½ teaspoon dried leaf sage**
> **½ cup apple cider**
> **1½ tablespoons cider vinegar**

1. Season the pork chops on both sides with salt and pepper. In a large skillet, heat the oil. Add the chops and cook over medium-high heat, turning once, for about 4 minutes per side, until browned. Using tongs, transfer the chops to a plate and set aside.

2. In the skillet drippings, cook the apple and onion over medium-low heat, stirring occasionally, for about 4 minutes, until the onion is just softened. Stir in the sage, cider, and vinegar.

3. Return the chops to the skillet along with any accumulated juices. Spoon the onion mixture over the chops. Cover

and cook over medium-low heat for 20 to 25 minutes, until the chops have no trace of pink at the center and are very tender. Season the sauce with additional salt and pepper to taste. Serve the chops with the onion and apple mixture spooned on top.

GARLIC-STEAMED SWISS CHARD

Makes 4 servings

1 pound Swiss chard
2 tablespoons olive oil
1 large garlic clove, minced
¼ teaspoon salt
¼ teaspoon black pepper

1. Trim the Swiss chard to separate the stems from the leaves. Thinly slice both the leaves and stems.

2. Heat the oil in a large skillet or 3-quart saucepan. Add the garlic and cook over medium-low heat for 30 seconds. Add the Swiss chard stems, cover the pan, and cook over low heat for 4 minutes. Add the leaves, cover the pan, and cook 3 to 5 minutes longer, until both the stems and leaves are tender. Season with the salt and pepper.

Devil's Food Cupcakes with Chocolate Satin Icing

Makes 12 cupcakes

Cupcakes
¼ teaspoon instant coffee

¼ cup very hot tap water

½ cup milk

1 egg

⅓ cup vegetable oil

¾ teaspoon vanilla extract

¾ cup all-purpose flour

⅔ cup granulated sugar

¼ cup unsweetened cocoa powder

¾ teaspoon baking powder

¾ teaspoon baking soda

¼ teaspoon salt

Chocolate Satin Icing
6 ounces semisweet chocolate chips (1 cup)

⅓ cup sour cream

½ teaspoon vanilla extract

⅓ cup confectioners' sugar

(continued on next page.)

(*continued*)

1. Preheat the oven to 350 degrees. Lightly grease 12 standard-size muffin tins, or line each with a paper cupcake liner.

2. To make the cupcakes, in a small bowl, dissolve the instant coffee in the hot water. Add the milk, then whisk in the egg until well blended. Finally beat in the oil and vanilla. Set aside.

3. In a large bowl, whisk or sift together the flour, granulated sugar, cocoa powder, baking powder, baking soda, and salt. Make a well in the center, then pour in the liquid ingredients. Whisk until smoothly blended.

4. Divide the batter among the cupcake tins, filling each about two-thirds full. Bake for 20 to 23 minutes, until the cupcakes have risen evenly and the tops spring back when touched. Let cool in the pans for 5 minutes, then turn out onto racks to cool completely.

5. For the frosting, melt the chocolate chips in the top of a double boiler or in a microwave oven. Let cool slightly, then whisk in the sour cream and vanilla. Beat in the confectioners' sugar until smooth. Let cool until thickened. Spread over tops of cupcakes.

CHICKEN HUNTER-STYLE*

◆

CREAMY POLENTA*

◆

CHICORY SALAD

◆

SHORTBREAD COOKIES

◆

Sunny Italy has a beautiful autumn season, and with it comes some wonderful traditional foods that are the inspiration for this menu. Adapted from the long-simmering Italian cacciatore, the main course is a streamlined chicken stew perfect for today's lighter taste and quick-cooking requirements. This saucy dish is perfectly teamed with creamy polenta, the smooth cornmeal pudding that is another Italian classic. (Polenta, by the way, is a wonderful, easily made starch that nicely complements almost any tomato-sauced dish.) A salad of chicory or a mix of bitter greens offers a crunchy contrast to this warming, comforting meal. Speaking of comforting, that is probably an apt adjective for the word "cookie," and shortbreads just might be the edible definition.

CHICKEN HUNTER-STYLE

Makes 4 servings

  1 pound skinless, boneless chicken breasts
  Salt and black pepper
  2 tablespoons olive oil
  1 large onion, chopped
  ½ pound mushrooms, sliced
  3 garlic cloves, minced
  1 (28-ounce) can tomatoes in puree
  ½ cup dry white wine
  1 bay leaf, broken in half
  1½ teaspoons dried marjoram
  ½ teaspoon grated lemon zest

1. Flatten the chicken breasts slightly with the heel of your hand. Season them lightly with salt and pepper. Heat the oil in a large skillet. Add the chicken breasts and cook over medium-high heat, turning once, for 2 to 3 minutes per side, until nicely browned. Using tongs, remove the chicken to a plate.

2. Add the onion, mushrooms, and garlic to the drippings in the skillet. Cook over medium heat, stirring often, for 5 minutes, or until the vegetables are softened. Add the to-

matoes with their juices, the wine, bay leaf, and marjoram. Reduce the heat to low and simmer, partially covered, for 10 minutes. Return the chicken and any accumulated juices to the pan. Simmer, uncovered, for about 10 minutes longer, until the sauce is somewhat thickened and the chicken is white and tender throughout. Discard the bay leaf and stir in the lemon zest before serving.

CREAMY POLENTA

Makes 4 servings

> 1¼ **cups yellow cornmeal**
> ½ **teaspoon salt, or more to taste**
> ⅛ **teaspoon black pepper, or more to taste**
> ⅓ **cup grated Parmesan cheese**

1. Bring 2½ cups of water to a boil in a large, heavy saucepan. In a medium bowl, whisk the cornmeal into 1½ cups cold water. Gradually whisk the cornmeal paste into the boiling water.

2. Simmer, uncovered, over low heat for 10 to 12 minutes, whisking often, until very thick. Whisk in the salt, pepper, and cheese. Serve at once.

SPAGHETTINI WITH SAVORY
BEAN SAUCE*

GARLIC BREAD

MIXED GREEN SALAD

BAKED SPICED APPLES*

Cost-conscious cooks in many cultures have been teaming pasta with beans for centuries. It is both satisfying and comforting. In addition, nutritionists tell us that eating more starch and less meat is definitely a health plus. All these facts are important, but perhaps the most compelling reason for trying this menu is that it tastes terrific and is easy to make. Canned beans are a great shortcut in the rich and savory sauce. And nicely spiced apples are sure to be popular with the entire family. Cortland, Rome Beauty, and Golden Delicious are good varieties for baking. Enough said.

Spaghettini with Savory Bean Sauce

Makes 4 servings

4 slices of bacon, cooked and crumbled
1 large onion, coarsely chopped
1 green bell pepper, coarsely chopped
1 large garlic clove, minced
2 (14- to 16-ounce) cans stewed tomatoes with their
   juices
1 (14- to 16-ounce) can white cannellini beans,
   drained
1 teaspoon dried oregano
1 teaspoon dried basil
½ teaspoon dried thyme
½ teaspoon salt
¼ teaspoon black pepper
12 ounces spaghettini or thin spaghetti
¼ cup grated Parmesan cheese (optional)

1. In a large skillet or flameproof casserole, fry the bacon over medium heat, turning, until it is crisp. Remove from the skillet and drain well on paper towels. Crumble and reserve the bacon.

(*continued on next page*)

(*continued*)

2. Add the onion, green pepper, and garlic to the skillet drippings. Cook over medium-low heat, stirring often, for about 5 minutes, until the vegetables are tender.

3. Add the tomatoes with their juices, the drained beans, and the oregano, basil, thyme, salt, and pepper to the skillet. Simmer, partially covered, over low heat for 15 minutes, until slightly thickened. (If the sauce becomes too thick, add a small amount of water, tomato juice, or wine.) Season with additional salt and pepper to taste.

4. Meanwhile, cook the pasta in a large pot of boiling salted water for 9 to 10 minutes, or until *al dente,* tender but firm. Drain well.

5. To serve, stir the bacon into the sauce, then ladle the sauce over the spaghettini. Sprinkle with the cheese, if desired.

BAKED SPICED APPLES

Makes 4 servings

> 4 small to medium baking apples (about 1½ pounds
>   total)
> 2 tablespoons butter, softened
> 2 tablespoons brown sugar
> ¼ teaspoon ground ginger
> ¼ teaspoon ground cinnamon
> ⅛ teaspoon ground cloves
> 1 tablespoon honey
> 1 teaspoon lemon juice

1. Preheat the oven to 375 degrees. Butter a baking dish just large enough to hold the apples in a single layer.

2. Core the apples and peel about one third of the way down. Arrange close together, but not touching, in the baking dish.

3. In a small bowl, combine the butter, brown sugar, ginger, cinnamon, and cloves. Blend well. Fill each apple core cavity with one-fourth of the spiced butter.

(*continued on next page*)

(*continued*)

4. In a small saucepan, combine the honey, lemon juice, and ½ cup of water. Bring just to a simmer, stirring to melt the honey. Pour the syrup over and around the apples.

5. Bake for 40 minutes, or until the apples are just fork-tender. Serve slightly warm in rimmed dishes with the syrup spooned over the apples.

PENNE WITH BROCCOLI RABE AND GARLIC*

◆

SEEDED BREAD STICKS

◆

RADICCHIO AND LEAF LETTUCE WITH BALSAMIC VINAIGRETTE*

◆

CARAMELIZED PEARS AND SPICED ICE CREAM*

◆

Ingredients that used to be considered exotic and foreign, such as broccoli rabe and radicchio, are now readily available to home cooks. Broccoli rabe looks like a weedy broccoli, with long stalks, dark green leaves, and yellowish-green buds. It tastes a lot like its namesake vegetable, but has sharp overtones of spring greens. Radicchio is a brilliant ruby-red member of the lettuce family that adds both a slightly bitter flavor and a decorative color accent. Ice cream was brought to this country by Thomas Jefferson so long ago that we consider it an all-American dessert. Spiced and topped with caramelized pears, it goes international.

PENNE WITH BROCCOLI RABE
AND GARLIC

Makes 4 servings

> 1 pound broccoli rabe
> 1 pound penne or other thick tubular pasta
> ¼ cup plus 2 tablespoons olive oil
> 3 large garlic cloves, minced
> 6 anchovies, finely chopped (optional)
> ½ teaspoon black pepper
> ½ cup crumbled feta cheese (2 ounces)

1. Wash the broccoli rabe well to rid it of any grit or sand, then cut it into 1½-inch lengths, including leaves, buds, and all but the tough very bottom stems.

2. Cook the pasta in a large pot of boiling salted water for 8 minutes. Add the broccoli rabe and cook for another 3 minutes, until both the pasta and vegetable are *al dente*, tender but firm. Ladle out ¾ cup of the pasta cooking water and reserve. Drain the pasta and greens into a colander.

3. While the pasta is cooking, heat the olive oil in a small skillet. Add the garlic and optional anchovies and cook over low heat for 2 minutes, mashing the anchovies.

4. In a large bowl, toss the pasta and greens with the garlic sauce and the reserved cooking water. Add the black pepper and the cheese and toss again gently to combine them.

RADICCHIO AND LEAF LETTUCE
WITH BALSAMIC VINAIGRETTE

Makes 4 servings

Radicchio is admittedly expensive, but a little goes a long way. Think of it as a salad accent, almost like a colorful fresh herb. If the price is prohibitive in your market, substitute red cabbage.

BALSAMIC VINAIGRETTE
3 tablespoons balsamic vinegar
1 teaspoon Dijon mustard
¼ teaspoon salt
⅛ teaspoon black pepper
¼ cup plus 2 tablespoons olive oil

SALAD
1 small head of radicchio
1 small head of green leaf lettuce

(continued on next page)

(*continued*)

1. To make the vinaigrette, whisk together the vinegar, mustard, salt, and pepper in a small bowl. Slowly whisk in the oil until blended.

2. For the salad, tear the radicchio and leaf lettuce into bite-sized pieces and place in a salad bowl. Drizzle the vinaigrette over the salad and toss to coat.

CARAMELIZED PEARS AND SPICED ICE CREAM

Makes 4 servings

> 2 cups vanilla ice cream or frozen yogurt (1 pint)
> ½ teaspoon ground allspice
> ¼ teaspoon ground cinnamon
> ⅛ teaspoon ground cloves
> 4 tablespoons (½ stick) butter
> 3 firm pears, cored, peeled, and thinly sliced
> 2 tablespoons lemon juice
> ¼ cup packed light brown sugar
> 2 tablespoons brandy or orange juice

1. Put the ice cream in a mixing bowl and let it sit at room temperature or place in a microwave oven for a few seconds until it is slightly softened. Add the allspice, cinnamon, and cloves and stir to blend well. Return the ice cream to the freezer until it firms up again and you are ready to use it, up to 2 days.

2. In a large skillet, melt the butter. Add the pears and sauté over medium-high heat, stirring often, for about 5 minutes, until slightly softened and beginning to brown. Stir in the lemon juice, then sprinkle on the brown sugar. Cook, stirring and mashing any lumps of sugar, for about 3 minutes longer, until the pears are tender and the brown sugar is dissolved into a lightly caramelized syrup. Remove the skillet from the heat and stir in the brandy. Return to the stove and simmer for 30 seconds.

3. To serve, divide the ice cream among 4 bowls. Ladle on the warm pears and sauce.

PEPPERY "FRIED" DRUMSTICKS*

◆

STEWED TOMATOES

◆

GLAZED ACORN SQUASH RINGS*

◆

RICE PUDDING

◆

This menu is designed to make economical use of some of
fall's simplest ingredients for an exceptionally savory and
satisfying supper on a cool autumn night. If you wish, the
squash rings can bake along with the chicken, or you can
cook them in a microwave oven. Finally, turn on the
broiler and finish the squash. The added bonus to this
oven-cooked meal is the wealth of wonderful aromas that
will fill your kitchen during the couple of hours that the
oven is quietly baking your dinner. Good smells are always
guaranteed to bring folks to the table at the first call, so be
ready for a quick seating.

Peppery "Fried" Drumsticks

Makes 4 servings

This "fried" chicken is really baked. The result is just as crispy and crunchy, but without all the fuss, mess, or fat.

3 tablespoons vegetable oil
1 tablespoon butter
½ teaspoon Tabasco or other hot pepper sauce
⅓ cup yellow cornmeal
¼ cup unseasoned dry bread crumbs
2 tablespoons all-purpose flour
½ teaspoon salt
¼ teaspoon cayenne
8 chicken drumsticks (about 1¾ pounds)

1. Preheat the oven to 125 degrees. Meanwhile, place the oil, butter, and Tabasco sauce in a 9-by-13-inch baking pan and set it in the oven briefly to melt the butter.

2. In a large plastic or paper bag, shake together the cornmeal, bread crumbs, flour, salt, and cayenne. Roll the chicken drumsticks in the melted oil and butter to coat all sides. Then toss, 2 pieces at a time, in the bag containing

the cornmeal coating. Place the chicken in a single layer in the baking pan, leaving a small space in between each piece.

3. Bake for about 30 minutes, until the chicken is golden brown, crispy, and cooked through with no trace of pink near the bone. Serve hot or at warm room temperature. Additional Tabasco or hot sauce can be passed at the table to shake on the chicken if you really like it hot.

GLAZED ACORN SQUASH RINGS

Makes 4 servings

The microwave oven is particularly well suited to cooking winter squash. Conventional instructions are given in a note at the end of the recipe.

2 small acorn squash (12 to 16 ounces each)
¼ teaspoon salt
⅛ teaspoon black pepper
1 tablespoon butter
1½ tablespoons molasses

1. Cut the top and bottom off each of the squash. Cut each squash crosswise into ½-inch-thick slices. Use a small knife or a small biscuit cutter to cut a round from the center of each slice to remove and discard the seeds.

2. To cook in a microwave oven, place the squash rings in a single, slightly overlapping layer in a buttered microwave-safe 2-quart shallow baking dish. Season with the salt and pepper. Cover the dish with plastic wrap. Cook on High, rearranging squash rings once, about 4 minutes, until tender. Let stand for 5 minutes. Drain off any excess liquid from the pan.

3. Preheat the broiler. Melt the butter with the molasses and brush the mixture over the cooked squash rings. Broil the squash 3 to 4 inches from the heat source for about 2 minutes, until glazed and the edges have golden-brown tinges. Serve directly from the baking dish or arrange on plates.

NOTE: To cook the squash in a conventional oven, preheat the oven to 425 degrees. Arrange the squash rings in a single, slightly overlapping layer in a 2-quart baking dish. Cover with foil and bake for about 25 minutes, until the squash is tender. Glaze as directed in step 3 above.

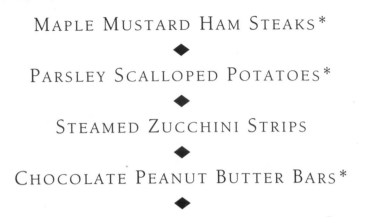

MAPLE MUSTARD HAM STEAKS*

◆

PARSLEY SCALLOPED POTATOES*

◆

STEAMED ZUCCHINI STRIPS

◆

CHOCOLATE PEANUT BUTTER BARS*

◆

In New England, the annual tapping of the maple trees signals that spring will come once again to the wintry, leafless landscape. Though maple syrup is always welcome over a stack of hot pancakes, it is put to somewhat more sophisticated use here in a lightly herbed sweet and sour glaze for ham steak. Similarly, salty ham always seems to cry out for a soothing, creamy complement, and scalloped potatoes fill the bill nicely. Steamed zucchini strips offer both good color and taste to round out the main course. America's favorite combination of chocolate and peanut butter make a welcome dessert any season of the year.

Maple Mustard Ham Steaks

Makes 4 servings

Canadian-style bacon can be used in place of ham steak.

- ¼ **cup maple syrup**
- **4 teaspoons Dijon or grainy mustard**
- **1 tablespoon cider vinegar**
- ¼ **teaspoon dried thyme leaves**
- ¼ **teaspoon black pepper**
- **1 pound center-cut ham steak**

1. Preheat the broiler. In a small dish, stir together the maple syrup, mustard, vinegar, and thyme.

2. Sprinkle the pepper over the ham, then place the steak on a rack in a broiler pan. Brush some of the maple syrup mixture over the ham. Broil about 4 inches from the heat source for 2 minutes. Brush with more of the maple glaze and broil 1 minute. Turn, brush with more glaze, and broil 2 minutes. Brush again with glaze and broil 1 minute longer, or until the ham is fully heated and golden.

3. Brush the ham steak with any remaining glaze, cut into 4 pieces, and serve.

PARSLEY SCALLOPED POTATOES

Makes 4 servings

2 tablespoons all-purpose flour
¾ teaspoon salt
¼ teaspoon black pepper
¼ cup chopped parsley
1½ pounds all-purpose or baking potatoes (3 or 4),
    peeled and thinly sliced
1 medium onion, thinly sliced
3 tablespoons butter
1¼ cups milk

1. Preheat the oven to 350 degrees. Generously butter a shallow 1½-quart casserole or baking dish. In a small dish, combine the flour, salt, pepper, and 3 tablespoons of the chopped parsley.

2. Cover the bottom of the baking dish with a layer of about one-third of the potatoes, then make a layer of about one-third of the onion. Sprinkle with about one-third of the flour mixture, then dot with about one-third of the butter. Make two more layers in the same manner to use all of the potatoes, onion, flour mixture, and butter. Pour the milk evenly over the potatoes.

3. Cover the casserole and bake for 35 minutes. Uncover, stir gently, and bake 30 to 40 minutes longer, until the potatoes are tender and the sauce is slightly thickened. If desired, the casserole can be glazed for a minute or so under the broiler until the potatoes are tinged golden brown.

4. Sprinkle the potatoes with the remaining 1 tablespoon parsley before serving.

CHOCOLATE PEANUT BUTTER BARS

Makes 16 to 24 cookies

Extra-chunky peanut butter is usually the same price as creamy, but offers a more interesting texture to this bar cookie. Either one can be used. Don't, however, use "natural" peanut butter, which tends to separate oil from solids upon standing. The dough can be made in a mixer or in a food processor.

(continued on next page)

(*continued*)

1 cup all-purpose flour

1 teaspoon baking powder

¼ teaspoon baking soda

⅔ cup peanut butter

4 tablespoons (½ stick) butter, softened

1 cup packed light brown sugar

2 eggs

1 teaspoon vanilla extract

6 ounces chocolate chips or mini-chips (1 cup)

1. Preheat the oven to 350 degrees. Grease an 8- or 9-inch square baking pan. Whisk or sift together the flour, baking powder, and baking soda.

2. In a mixing bowl or a food processor, cream together the peanut butter, butter, and brown sugar. Add the eggs and vanilla and blend until smooth. Add the flour mixture and mix or pulse until the batter is just blended and smooth. By hand or with a few pulses of the food processor, mix in the chocolate chips. Spread into the prepared pan.

3. Bake for 30 to 35 minutes, until the surface is dry and golden and a toothpick inserted in the center comes out nearly clean. Let cool completely in the pan on a rack. To serve, cut in 16 to 24 bars. Store extra bars airtight at room temperature for about 3 days or freeze for up 1 to month.

Basque Chicken and Rice with Olives *

♦

Green Salad

♦

Spiced Oranges *

♦

Brown Sugar Almond Wafers *

♦

Basque cooking may sound exotic, but it is some of the finest, most down-to-earth home cooking on the Iberian peninsula. The Basques, who occupy the northernmost regions of Spain, are passionate about food. With assertive spices and herbs, they transform the simplest of ingredient combinations into memorable dishes. Chicken and rice, for example, is made special with olive oil and good Spanish olives. Oranges and almonds, other important ingredients in Spanish cooking, are especially pleasing in tandem, such as in this dessert duet of gently spiced oranges accompanied by thin, crisp almond wafers.

BASQUE CHICKEN AND RICE WITH OLIVES

Makes 4 servings

The size of the olives is not important here, so don't pay a premium for jumbo. The recipe is most economical made with a cut-up chicken. If your can of chicken broth is slightly less than 2 cups, make up the remainder with water.

2½ to 3 pounds cut-up chicken parts
¼ teaspoon cayenne
2 tablespoons olive oil
3 ounces smoked ham, diced (¾ cup)
1 medium onion, coarsely chopped
1 medium green bell pepper, coarsely chopped
2 garlic cloves, minced
1 cup long-grain white rice
2 cups chicken broth
¾ cup sliced pimiento-stuffed green olives
Salt and black pepper

1. Season the chicken with the cayenne. Heat the oil in a large skillet, add the chicken, and cook over medium heat, turning occasionally, for about 10 minutes, until golden brown. Use tongs to remove the chicken from the skillet.

2. Add the ham, onion, green pepper, and garlic to the drippings in the skillet. Cook over medium heat, stirring often, for about 5 minutes, until the vegetables are softened and the ham is lightly browned. Add the rice and cook about 30 seconds, stirring to coat the rice with the vegetables and oil. Stir in the chicken broth.

3. Return the chicken to the skillet. Cover and simmer over low heat for 20 minutes. Add the olives and stir gently to distribute them fairly well. Cover the skillet and simmer 2 minutes longer, or until the rice is tender and the liquid has been absorbed. Season with salt and pepper to taste.

SPICED ORANGES

Makes 4 servings

- **4 small seedless oranges**
- **1 lemon**
- **⅓ cup sugar**
- **1 cup water**
- **1 cinnamon stick**
- **4 whole allspice berries**

(continued on next page)

(*continued*)

1. Use a small, sharp knife to peel eight ½-inch by 2-inch strips from one of the oranges and 4 similarly sized strips from the lemon. Then peel the oranges, removing the white pith. Cut the fruit crosswise into ½-inch-thick slices and place in a heatproof bowl. (Cut the fruit over the bowl in order to catch and reserve the juice.) Squeeze 1½ tablespoons juice from the lemon, and reserve.

2. Place the sugar and water in a small saucepan. Break the cinnamon stick both lengthwise and crosswise in half to make 4 pieces. Add the cinnamon stick pieces and the allspice to the saucepan. Slowly bring the mixture to a boil, stirring to dissolve the sugar completely. Lower the heat and simmer for 3 minutes.

3. Pour the simmering spice syrup over the oranges in the bowl. Stir in the lemon juice. Let cool and refrigerate at least 3 hours or up to 8 hours.

4. To serve, use a slotted spoon to divide the oranges and spices among 4 dessert bowls. Spoon the syrup over the oranges.

Brown Sugar Almond Wafers

Makes about 5 dozen

⅓ cup chopped, slivered, or sliced almonds
1 cup all-purpose flour
½ cup packed brown sugar
¼ cup granulated sugar
½ teaspoon baking powder
⅛ teaspoon salt
6 tablespoons (¾ stick) butter
1 egg
¼ teaspoon vanilla extract
¼ teaspoon almond extract

1. Lightly toast the almonds on a baking sheet in a 350 degree oven for about 5 minutes, stirring often. Or toast them in a microwave oven on High for about 4 minutes, stirring 2 or 3 times. Let the nuts cool completely.

2. In a food processor, finely chop the nuts. Add the flour, brown sugar, granulated sugar, baking powder, and salt. Process 15 seconds, or until well blended. Cut the butter into about 12 pieces and distribute over the flour mixture. Pulse to cut in the butter until the pieces are the size of

small peas. In a small bowl, lightly beat the egg with the vanilla and almond extract. With the machine on, pour the egg mixture through the feed tube and process until the dough just gathers together into clumps.

3. Scrape the dough out onto a large piece of plastic wrap or waxed paper. Shape into a log 1¾ inches in diameter. Refrigerate until firm, at least 1 hour or up to 24 hours.

4. Preheat the oven to 400 degrees. Lightly grease a large baking sheet.

5. Cut the dough log crosswise in half. Keeping one part refrigerated, use a sharp knife to slice the remaining dough into ⅛-inch-thick rounds. Place the rounds, 1 inch apart, on the baking sheet. Bake 7 minutes, or until the edges of the cookies are lightly browned. Use a spatula to remove the cookies to a rack to cool completely. Repeat to use the remaining dough. Store the cookies in an airtight container up to 3 days or freeze up to 1 month.

NOTE: To make the dough in a mixer, finely chop the nuts by hand. Whisk or sift together the flour, baking powder, and salt. Then cream the butter with the brown sugar and granulated sugar until smooth. Beat in the egg, vanilla, and almond extract, then blend in the flour mixture and the nuts. Chill, slice, and bake as directed above.

Winter

◆

The northern world may lie snow covered in winter, but in the tropics a veritable explosion of seasonal abundance is just beginning. Oranges, lemons, tangerines, and grapefruit arrive swiftly and economically in markets thousands of miles away. All sorts of other tropical delectables are available and at their most affordable now. Depending upon the shipment of the week, pineapples or mangoes, avocados or bananas can be good buys.

Brilliant red cranberries, the all-American fruit of the season, are a hearty crop, and tradition ensures that they are available and well priced from late October through December. (Always buy a few extra bags and toss them in the freezer, because when the season is over, these little gems can cost almost as much as real rubies.)

Whole turkeys, always a reasonably good buy, hold their very best prices throughout the holiday season. If you can't use a whole bird at one time, ask the butcher to cut one up into parts—drumsticks, breast, and thighs, with carcass and giblets saved for soup. Because this is the season for parties, ice cream and cookies are often featured as specials, as are fancy cuts of meat, such as pork or chicken cutlets. These can be the basis of elegant, quick meals, ideas for which can be found throughout this book

TURKEY PICCATA*

◆

GARLIC ORZO WITH CARROTS AND MARJORAM*

◆

BROCCOLI SPEARS

◆

CRANBERRY CLAFOUTI*

◆

Instead of expensive veal, this piccata ` made with less costly turkey breast cutlets. The piquant lemony main course is nicely complemented by orzo, rice-shaped pasta, tossed with garlic, grated carrot, and marjoram. Spears of beautiful bright green broccoli add just the right color and flavor. The dessert, which is a take-off on a French country classic that traditionally calls for cherries, takes advantage here of the seasonal availability of tart fresh cranberries.

TURKEY PICCATA

Makes 4 servings

Chicken breast cutlets can easily be substituted for the turkey, if you like.

   1 pound boneless turkey cutlets
   ⅓ cup all-purpose flour
   ½ teaspoon salt
   ¼ teaspoon black pepper
   ¼ cup olive oil
   ¾ cup dry white wine
   1 tablespoon lemon juice
   ½ teaspoon grated lemon zest
   4 thin slices of lemon
   1 tablespoon chopped parsley

1. Place the cutlets on a work surface, cover with a sheet of plastic wrap, and pound with a mallet or the bottom of a heavy saucepan to flatten to about ¼ inch thick. Combine the flour, salt, and pepper on a plate. Coat both sides of the cutlets with the seasoned flour, shaking off the excess.

(*continued on next page*)

(*continued*)

2. Heat the oil in a large skillet and sauté the turkey over medium-high heat for about 2 minutes on the first side and 1 minute on the second side, until the meat is no longer pink. (You may need to do this in two batches.) Remove to a plate.

3. Add the wine and lemon juice to the drippings in the skillet, bring to a boil, and simmer, uncovered, stirring to dissolve the browned bits in the bottom of the pan, until the sauce is slightly reduced and thickened, about 2 minutes. Stir in the lemon zest.

4. Return the turkey and any juices that have accumulated on the plate to the skillet, add the lemon slices and parsley, and heat through.

GARLIC ORZO WITH CARROTS
AND MARJORAM

Makes 4 servings

 1 cup orzo (about 8 ounces)
 2 tablespoons olive oil
 2 garlic cloves, minced
 1 small carrot, peeled and grated
 ½ teaspoon dried marjoram
 ½ teaspoon salt
 ¼ teaspoon black pepper

1. Bring a large pot of salted water to a boil for the pasta. Cook the orzo for about 10 minutes, or until *al dente*, tender but firm. Drain into a sieve.

2. Meanwhile, heat the oil in a small skillet. Add the garlic and cook over low heat for about 2 minutes, until slightly softened and very lightly browned.

3. Return the orzo to the cooking pot set over low heat and add the garlic oil, the carrot, and marjoram. Toss until heated through. Season with salt and pepper before serving.

CRANBERRY CLAFOUTI

Makes 4 servings

3 eggs
½ cup granulated sugar
½ cup all-purpose flour
1 cup milk
2 teaspoons vanilla extract
1 cup fresh cranberries
Confectioners' sugar, for dusting
½ cup heavy cream (optional)

1. In a mixing bowl, whisk together the eggs and sugar until well blended. Add the flour and whisk until blended. Gradually whisk in the milk and add the vanilla.

2. Preheat the oven to 350 degrees. Generously butter an 8-inch square or other 1-quart baking dish and scatter the cranberries over the bottom of the dish.

3. Whisk the custard briefly to blend and slowly pour it over the cranberries. Bake for 45 to 50 minutes, until the *clafouti* is puffed and a rich golden brown color. Remove from the oven and dust heavily with confectioners' sugar. Serve immediately, with a pitcher of cream on the side.

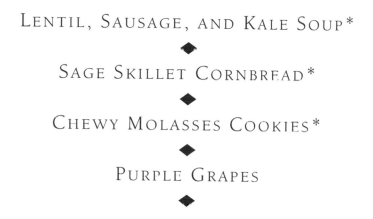

Lentil, Sausage, and Kale Soup*

◆

Sage Skillet Cornbread*

◆

Chewy Molasses Cookies*

◆

Purple Grapes

◆

What could be better on a chilly winter night than a bowl of hearty soup? This one, made with a base of healthful and economical quick-cooking lentils, is a true meal-in-a-bowl. Wedges of crusty golden sage-scented cornbread are a welcome accompaniment. For dessert, these old-fashioned chewy molasses cookies will perfume the kitchen with their fragrant spices.

LENTIL, SAUSAGE, AND KALE SOUP

Makes 4 servings

This soup is delicious made with either brown or green lentils.

3 tablespoons olive oil

1 onion, chopped

1 celery stalk, chopped

2 cups chicken broth

1½ cups (about 10 ounces) lentils, rinsed and
   picked over to remove any grit

1 bay leaf

¼ teaspoon dried hot pepper flakes

½ pound kale

12 ounces kielbasa or other garlicky smoked cooked
   sausage

1 (16-ounce) can plum tomatoes, with their juice

2 teaspoons red wine vinegar

½ teaspoon salt, or to taste

¼ teaspoon black pepper, or to taste

1. Heat the oil in a large kettle or soup pot. Cook the onion and celery over medium-low heat until they begin to soften, about 4 minutes. Add 6 cups of water and the broth, lentils, bay leaf, and hot pepper. Bring to a boil, lower the heat, and simmer, partially covered, until the lentils are almost tender, about 30 minutes.

2. Meanwhile, wash the kale, discarding the stems and tough ribs, and thinly slice the leaves. Slice the sausage into ½-inch rounds. Add the kale, sausage, and canned tomatoes with their juice to the soup. Bring to a simmer, breaking up the tomatoes with the side of a spoon, and cook, uncovered, for 15 minutes longer. If the soup is too thick, add up to 1 cup or so more water. Stir in the vinegar and season with salt and pepper. (The amount of salt will depend on the saltiness of the sausage.)

3. Ladle into large soup bowls to serve.

SAGE SKILLET CORNBREAD

Makes about 6 servings

1¼ cups all-purpose flour
¾ cup yellow cornmeal
2 tablespoons sugar
1 tablespoon baking powder
¾ teaspoon salt
½ teaspoon dried sage
1 egg
1 cup milk
¼ cup vegetable oil

1. Preheat the oven to 400 degrees. Grease a black cast-iron skillet that measures approximately 10 inches across the top and 8½ inches across the bottom (or a 9-inch square baking pan). In a bowl, stir together the flour, cornmeal, sugar, baking powder, salt, and sage until well blended.

2. In a small bowl, whisk together the egg, milk, and oil. Pour the liquid ingredients into the dry and mix just until blended. Spread the batter into the prepared pan and bake for 18 to 20 minutes, until the top is a pale, golden brown and a skewer inserted in the center of the bread comes out clean. Cut into wedges to serve.

CHEWY MOLASSES COOKIES

Makes about 2 dozen

This cookie dough can also be made in a food processor. Be sure, though, to thoroughly mix the flour with the spices before adding it to the work bowl.

8 tablespoons (1 stick) butter, softened
¾ cup granulated sugar
1 egg
½ cup molasses
2 cups all-purpose flour
½ teaspoon baking soda
½ teaspoon salt
¾ teaspoon ground ginger
½ teaspoon ground cinnamon
½ teaspoon grated nutmeg

1. Using an electric mixer, cream the butter and ½ cup of the sugar until smooth. Beat in the egg and molasses.

2. Sift or mix together the flour, baking soda, salt, ginger, cinnamon, and nutmeg. With the mixer on low speed, add the spiced flour to the dough and mix just until combined.

(continued on next page)

(*continued*)

Shape the dough into a flattened disk, wrap in plastic wrap, and refrigerate for at least 30 minutes or for up to 24 hours.

3. Preheat the oven to 350 degrees. Place the remaining ¼ cup of sugar in a small dish.

4. Pinch off small pieces of the dough and roll them into balls about 1 inch in diameter. Roll each ball in the sugar and place 2 inches apart on lightly greased cookie sheets.

5. Bake for 12 to 14 minutes, until the tops are rounded and crinkled and the cookies are set. Remove from the sheets and let cool on a rack. Store in a tightly covered container for a few days or freeze for up to 1 month.

THYME-ROASTED GAME HENS*

◆

CARAMELIZED WINTER VEGETABLES*

◆

CELERY RICE PILAF*

◆

FROZEN LEMON YOGURT

◆

Whether the vegetables roast alongside the game hens or in a separate pan, this dinner sends off irresistibly tantalizing aromas from the oven as it cooks. Carrots, turnips, and onions are particularly good for roasting because they're low in moisture but high in sugar, which allows them to caramelize beautifully as they cook. Chopped celery, which is added to the rice pilaf, contributes yet another savory dimension. Frozen yogurt is nice to have on hand as a refreshing dessert to serve after many meals, and if purchased in the half-gallon size, it is quite economical.

THYME-ROASTED GAME HENS

Makes 4 servings

2 Cornish game hens (about 1¾ pounds each)
Salt and black pepper
2 tablespoons olive oil
1 teaspoon dried thyme

1. Preheat the oven to 400 degrees. Pull any excess fat off the game hens and season the cavities lightly with salt and pepper. Tie the legs together with string and place the birds in a large, shallow roasting pan, not touching one another. Brush or drizzle with the oil and sprinkle with the thyme and salt and pepper.

2. Roast for 10 minutes. Reduce the heat to 350 degrees and continue cooking for about 40 minutes, until the thigh juices run clear when pierced with a sharp knife. Baste with the pan juices 2 or 3 times during roasting.

3. Remove the hens from the roasting pan and skim the fat off the pan juices. Discard the strings and with a large knife, cut each bird in half, discarding the backbones. Place a half on each plate and spoon the pan juices on top.

CARAMELIZED WINTER VEGETABLES

Makes 4 servings

1 pound carrots
1 pound white turnips
1 medium onion
1½ tablespoons olive oil
½ teaspoon salt
¼ teaspoon black pepper
Pinch of sugar

1. Preheat the oven to 400 degrees. Peel the carrots and turnips. Cut the carrots into 2½- to 3-inch lengths, and slice the thick ends lengthwise. Cut the turnips into 2-inch chunks. Cut the onion into thick slices.

2. Combine the vegetables in a large shallow roasting pan or rimmed baking sheet. Drizzle with the oil, tossing to coat, and sprinkle with the salt, pepper, and sugar.

3. Roast, uncovered, for 10 minutes. Reduce the heat to 350 degrees and cook for about 40 minutes, until the onion is soft and the root vegetables are tender and nicely browned. Turn once during cooking with tongs or a spatula.

CELERY RICE PILAF

Makes 4 servings

Nice fresh celery will turn this rice dish a beautiful pale green in color.

- **2 tablespoons butter**
- **1 small onion, chopped**
- **1 large celery stalk, chopped**
- **1 cup long-grain white rice**
- **2 cups chicken broth or a mixture of broth and water**
- **3 tablespoons chopped parsley**
- **Salt to taste**

1. Heat the butter in a heavy medium saucepan. Add the onion and celery and cook over medium heat for 3 minutes. Add the rice and cook, stirring, for 2 minutes, until the grains are coated with butter. Add the chicken broth and stir once with a fork. Cover the pot and cook the rice over very low heat for about 18 minutes, until the grains are tender.

2. Fluff the rice with a fork, stir in the parsley, and season with salt to taste. (The amount of salt needed will depend on the saltiness of the chicken broth.)

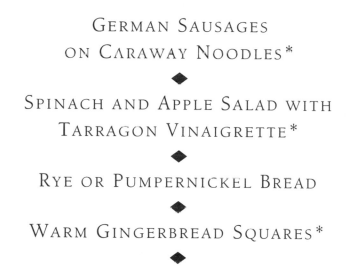

GERMAN SAUSAGES
ON CARAWAY NOODLES*

◆

SPINACH AND APPLE SALAD WITH
TARRAGON VINAIGRETTE*

◆

RYE OR PUMPERNICKEL BREAD

◆

WARM GINGERBREAD SQUARES*

◆

Inspired by Alsatian *choucroute garnie,* the centerpiece dish
of this menu uses traditional European-style sausages, but
calls for quick-cooking Savoy (or curly) cabbage instead of
sauerkraut, and adds egg noodles for substance. Serve
good mustard and some dark bread on the side, along with
this spinach salad, which is enlivened by the addition of a
little thinly sliced sweet apple and onion. A square of
fragrant, pleasantly sticky, dark gingerbread, warm from
the oven, provides the perfect finish.

GERMAN SAUSAGES
ON CARAWAY NOODLES

Makes 4 servings

You could also use breakfast sausage links in this recipe. Just be sure to simmer them a little longer to make sure they get cooked through.

    1 pound German or Polish sausages (smoked or
        unsmoked), such as bratwurst, weisswurst, or
        kielbasa
    2 tablespoons vegetable oil
    1 medium onion, chopped
    4 cups thinly sliced Savoy cabbage (9 to 10 ounces)
    ½ cup dry white wine
    1 teaspoon dried thyme
    ¾ teaspoon caraway seed
    1 cup whipping cream or heavy cream
    12 ounces wide egg noodles
    Black pepper and salt to taste

1. If the sausages are not in links, slice them into 3-inch lengths. Prick the sausages in several places with a fork. Heat the oil in a large skillet. Add the sausages and cook over medium-high heat, turning, until browned, about 5 minutes. Remove to a plate with tongs.

2. Add the onion to the skillet drippings and cook over medium heat for 2 minutes. Add the cabbage, wine, thyme, and caraway seed. Bring to a simmer, return the sausages and any accumulated juices to the skillet, cover, and cook over low heat until the sausages are heated through, about 10 minutes. Add the cream. Cook, uncovered, over medium-high heat for 1 to 2 minutes, until the sauce is slightly reduced and thickened. Set aside, covered to keep warm.

3. Cook the noodles in a large pot of boiling salted water for 7 to 8 minutes, until *al dente,* tender but firm.

4. Drain the noodles and transfer to a large platter. Spoon the cabbage cream sauce and sausages over the noodles. Season to taste with plenty of black pepper and salt if necessary.

SPINACH AND APPLE SALAD WITH TARRAGON VINAIGRETTE

Makes 4 servings

TARRAGON VINAIGRETTE
2 tablespoons tarragon-white wine vinegar
¾ teaspoon Dijon mustard
¼ teaspoon sugar
¼ teaspoon salt
⅛ teaspoon black pepper
¼ cup vegetable oil
2 tablespoons olive oil

SPINACH AND APPLE SALAD
10 ounces fresh spinach leaves (about 7 cups),
    washed, dried, and stems removed
½ cup thinly sliced sweet white onion
1 red Delicious apple

1. To make the vinaigrette, combine the vinegar, mustard, sugar, salt, and pepper in a jar or small bowl. Stir or whisk in the vegetable oil and olive oil.

2. For the salad, tear the spinach into bite-sized pieces and combine in a large salad bowl with the sliced onion. Just before serving, core the apple, cut into thin slices, and add to the spinach. Drizzle the dressing over the salad and toss.

WARM GINGERBREAD SQUARES

Makes 4 to 6 servings

This gingerbread is also wonderful eaten at room temperature out of hand as a snack.

½ cup molasses
¼ cup packed brown sugar, preferably dark brown
4 tablespoons (½ stick) butter
½ cup orange juice
1¼ cups all-purpose flour
1 teaspoon baking soda
1½ teaspoons ground ginger
½ teaspoon ground cinnamon
½ teaspoon grated nutmeg
¼ teaspoon ground cloves
1 egg
Whipped cream (optional)

(continued on next page)

(*continued*)

1. Preheat the oven to 375 degrees. Grease and flour an 8- or 9-inch square baking dish.

2. In a medium saucepan, combine the molasses, brown sugar, and butter. Cook over medium heat, stirring, until the butter is melted and the mixture is bubbly, about 2 minutes. Stir in the orange juice and set aside for a few minutes to cool.

3. In a bowl, sift or whisk together the flour, baking soda, ginger, cinnamon, nutmeg, and cloves.

4. When the molasses mixture is lukewarm, beat in the egg. Add the flour mixture and beat just until the flour is incorporated.

5. Pour the batter into the prepared pan and bake for 20 to 25 minutes, until the top is springy and a toothpick inserted in the center comes out clean. (The larger pan will take the shorter baking time.)

6. Serve the gingerbread warm, cut in squares, with a spoonful of whipped cream on top, if desired.

Tortilla Pizzas with Beef and Bean Topping*

◆

Avocado and Sweet Onion Salad*

◆

Tangerine Compote*

◆

Butter Cookies

◆

Tex-Mex food is always a pick-me-up in midwinter. Its spicy flavors and bright colors and textures are so lively that it can cheer most anyone right out of the gray-weather doldrums. These tortilla pizzas are similar to tostadas, except that they spend a brief time in the oven to melt the cheese on top, and the colorful avocado salad is served on the side. In the winter, avocados are plentiful and affordable. Look for fruit that just gives to gentle pressure when pressed.

To finish the meal, tangerines, a small, sweet variety of Mandarin orange, are sliced crosswise and tossed with a little sugar and liqueur to make a lovely compote. Pass a plate of butter cookies with the fruit.

Tortilla Pizzas with Beef and Bean Topping

Makes 4 servings

Corn tortillas would work well in this recipe, too, but since they are usually smaller, allow three per serving.

  ½ pound ground beef
  1 medium onion, chopped
  1 garlic clove, minced
  1 tablespoon chili powder
  ¾ teaspoon ground cumin
  ¾ teaspoon dried oregano
  ⅛ teaspoon cayenne, or more to taste
  1 (14- to 16-ounce) can pinto or kidney beans,
     drained
  8 (7- or 8-inch) flour tortillas
  2 cups grated Monterey Jack or mild Cheddar cheese
     (8 ounces)
  3 to 4 jalapeño peppers, seeded and chopped
  About ½ cup bottled salsa

1. In a large skillet, cook the beef and onion over medium heat, stirring to break up the meat, until the beef has lost its pink color, about 5 minutes. Add the garlic, chili powder, cumin, oregano, and cayenne and cook for 1 minute. Stir in the beans and about ¾ cup of water and simmer the mixture, partially covered, for 10 minutes. Uncover the skillet and cook over medium heat for 5 minutes, mashing about half of the beans against the side of the pan with a spoon to thicken the mixture. The topping should be quite thick but not sticking to the pan. Add a small amount of additional water if necessary. Spoon off any excess fat. (The topping can be made several hours ahead.)

2. Preheat the oven to 425 degrees. Place the tortillas in a single layer on 2 large baking sheets and bake for 2 to 3 minutes, until lightly toasted.

3. Divide the topping among the tortillas, spreading it almost to the edges. Sprinkle the cheese and chopped jalapeños over the beef and bean topping.

4. Bake the pizzas for 4 to 6 minutes, until the edges are crisp and the cheese is melted and bubbly.

5. To serve, cut into wedges. Pass the salsa at the table.

AVOCADO AND SWEET ONION SALAD

Makes 4 servings

LIME VINAIGRETTE
1 tablespoon white wine vinegar
1 tablespoon lime juice
½ teaspoon sugar
¼ teaspoon salt
⅛ teaspoon black pepper
6 tablespoons vegetable oil
1 teaspoon grated lime zest

AVOCADO AND ONION SALAD
Several leaves of lettuce, such as romaine or Boston
1 large avocado
¾ cup thinly sliced red onion

1. To make the vinaigrette, combine the vinegar, lime juice, sugar, salt, and pepper in a jar or small bowl. Stir or whisk in the oil and lime zest.

2. For the salad, line a serving platter or individual salad plates with lettuce leaves. Peel and pit the avocado and cut

into thin slices. Arrange in a decorative spoke pattern over the lettuce and scatter the onion over the avocado. Pour the dressing over the salad and serve.

TANGERINE COMPOTE

Makes 4 servings

Tangerines are ideal for this simple dessert because they are a good buy in the late fall and early winter, but tangelos, oranges, or even Clementines, if they keep to the budget, would taste wonderful, too.

4 tangerines
1 tablespoon sugar
2 tablespoons orange-flavored liqueur or dark rum

1. Peel the tangerines, poke out any seeds, and cut crosswise into slices with a sharp serrated knife.

2. Toss in a bowl with the sugar and liqueur or rum and let stand for about 15 minutes, until the sugar is dissolved.

3. Serve from an attractive glass bowl.

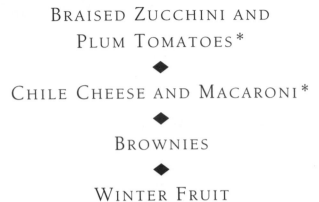

BRAISED ZUCCHINI AND
PLUM TOMATOES*

◆

CHILE CHEESE AND MACARONI*

◆

BROWNIES

◆

WINTER FRUIT

◆

While everyone knows that macaroni and cheese is a
budget meal-planner's delight, the concept is so appealing
that it merits some variations on the theme. This time, the
flavorings are slightly Tex-Mexican, with some chili
powder stirred into the sauce, as well as readily available
chopped green chiles and some diced smoked ham. A side
dish of ever-so-slightly-sweet braised tomatoes and
zucchini adds color and contrasting flavor to the dinner
plate. Pass a platter of fudgy brownies—homemade or
store-bought—and some winter fruit, such as pears or
tangerines, to eat out of hand for dessert.

Braised Zucchini and Plum Tomatoes

Makes 4 servings

1½ tablespoons olive oil
1 small onion, chopped
2 medium zucchini (about 6 ounces each), cut into
    ¼-inch-thick diagonal slices
6 plum tomatoes (about 1 pound), coarsely chopped
1 garlic clove, minced
½ teaspoon sugar
⅛ teaspoon ground cumin
¼ teaspoon salt
⅛ teaspoon black pepper

1. Heat the oil in a large skillet. Add the onion and zucchini and cook over medium-high heat, stirring occasionally, until the vegetables begin to brown lightly, about 5 minutes.

2. Add the tomatoes, garlic, sugar, cumin, salt, pepper, and ¼ cup of water. Cover and cook over low heat until the vegetables are softened, about 8 minutes. If the sauce is watery, raise the heat, uncover the pan, and cook for a minute or 2, until the sauce is reduced and thickened.

CHILE CHEESE AND MACARONI

Makes 4 servings

Here's a zesty macaroni and cheese that will brighten up the coldest winter night. For vegetarians, omit the ham or substitute cooked chicken or turkey.

  12 ounces ziti, rotelle, or other similar-size pasta
  3 tablespoons butter
  1 medium onion, chopped
  3 tablespoons all-purpose flour
  1 teaspoon chili powder
  2 cups milk
  2 cups grated Cheddar cheese (8 ounces)
  1 (4-ounce) can chopped green chiles, drained
  1 cup diced smoked ham (4 ounces)
  ½ teaspoon salt, or to taste
  ¼ teaspoon black pepper, or to taste

1. Cook the pasta in a large pot of boiling salted water for about 10 minutes, or until *al dente,* tender but firm. Drain into a colander.

2. Meanwhile, melt the butter in a large skillet, add the onion, and cook over medium-low heat until soft, about

5 minutes. Add the flour and chili powder and cook, stirring, for 2 minutes. Slowly whisk in the milk, then raise the
heat to medium and cook and stir until the mixture comes
to a boil and thickens. Cook for 1 minute. Remove the pan
from the heat and add the cheese, stirring until it is melted.
Stir in the chiles and ham.

3. Combine the sauce with the drained pasta and season to
taste with salt and black pepper. (The cheese, chiles, and
ham are salty, so the dish may not need much additional
salt.)

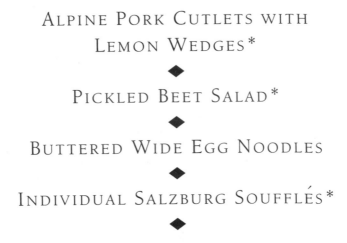

ALPINE PORK CUTLETS WITH LEMON WEDGES*

◆

PICKLED BEET SALAD*

◆

BUTTERED WIDE EGG NOODLES

◆

INDIVIDUAL SALZBURG SOUFFLÉS*

◆

Although originally made only with costly veal, *schnitzel* are now done in Austria with pork, too. Breaded with crumbs and gently fried, the cutlets are truly tasty in any language. Pork cutlets are available in most supermarkets. If you can't find them, thinly slice partially frozen boneless pork chops or substitute easily found chicken cutlets. In Austria, the traditional accompaniments often include a couple of side salads to balance the richness of the meat. This pickled beet salad adds color as well as contrasting flavor. Wide egg noodles tossed with butter complete the plate. And for dessert, serve light, lovely individual soufflés (or *Nockerln* in Salzburg), which, though they require a little last-minute attention, are the perfect finish to this Continental meal.

Alpine Pork Cutlets with Lemon Wedges

Makes 4 servings

3 tablespoons flour
¼ teaspoon salt
¼ teaspoon black pepper
1 egg
1¼ cups fresh bread crumbs
1 pound boneless pork cutlets, cut about
    ¼ inch thick
2 tablespoons butter
1 tablespoon vegetable oil
1 lemon, cut into quarters to make wedges

1. On a large plate, combine the flour, salt, and pepper. In a shallow dish, lightly beat the egg with 1 tablespoon of water. Spread the crumbs out on another plate.

2. Coat each cutlet with the seasoned flour, shaking off any excess. Dip in the egg, and then into the bread crumbs to coat completely. Pat the crumbs into the pork with your fingers so they adhere.

(*continued on next page*)

(*continued*)

3. Melt the butter in the oil in a large skillet over medium heat. Add the breaded cutlets and cook, turning once, for about 4 minutes per side, until the crust is golden brown and the meat is no longer pink when cut into with a knife. (This may need to be done in two batches.) Garnish with the lemon wedges before serving.

PICKLED BEET SALAD

Makes 4 servings

Although they don't have quite the same depth of flavor, canned beets would work fine in this recipe. Simply drain and marinate in the pickling liquid.

   1½ to 2 pounds beets
   ⅓ cup vinegar (any type)
   2 tablespoons sugar
   ¼ teaspoon salt
   ⅛ teaspoon celery seed
   8 to 12 romaine lettuce leaves
   2 tablespoons olive oil
   2 tablespoons minced scallions, including green tops

1. Cut off all but 1 inch of the beet tops. (The trimmed beets should weigh about 1 pound.) Rinse the beets well, but leave the skins on. Leave whole if the beets are of uniform size; cut large beets in half if sizes vary widely. Cook, uncovered, in a medium saucepan of lightly salted water to cover for 35 to 45 minutes, until tender when pierced with a knife. Drain, and when cool enough to handle, trim off the tops, slip off the skins, and cut the beets into thin slices. Put them in a medium-sized heatproof bowl.

2. In a small nonaluminum saucepan, bring the vinegar, sugar, salt, and celery seed to a boil. Reduce the heat and simmer for 1 minute.

3. Pour the hot liquid over the sliced beets and toss to coat. Refrigerate for at least 20 minutes to cool or for up to 3 days.

4. To serve, place the lettuce leaves on a large plate or divide among individual salad plates. Use a slotted spoon to remove the beets from their pickling liquid and spoon them over the lettuce. Drizzle the olive oil over the pickled beets and sprinkle the minced scallions on top.

INDIVIDUAL SALZBURG SOUFFLÉS

Makes 4 servings

Sliced strawberries are a nice, though certainly not necessary, addition on the plate.

  3 eggs, separated
  ⅛ teaspoon cream of tartar
  ¼ cup granulated sugar
  1½ tablespoons all-purpose flour
  1 teaspoon grated lemon zest
  1 teaspoon vanilla extract
  Confectioners' sugar, for dusting

1. Preheat the oven to 350 degrees. Butter a 9- or 10-inch pie plate or similar-size shallow baking dish.

2. Using an electric mixer, beat the egg whites until foamy. Add the cream of tartar and beat until soft peaks form. Beat in the granulated sugar, 1 tablespoon at a time, until the meringue is smooth and glossy.

3. In another bowl, using the same beaters or whisking by hand, beat the egg yolks for about 3 minutes, until they are light in color and form a ribbon when the beater is lifted. Sprinkle on the flour, lemon zest, and vanilla and beat just until blended.

4. Stir a heaping spoonful of the beaten egg whites into the yolks to lighten them, then fold the yolk mixture gently into the whites.

5. Using a large spoon, make 4 separate heaping mounds of the soufflé mixture in the baking dish. It is all right if the mounds touch each other.

6. Bake the soufflés in the lower center of the oven for 15 to 18 minutes, until puffed and golden brown on the outside. The centers should still be soft.

7. Dust liberally with confectioners' sugar. Serve immediately by separating the soufflés carefully with the tines of a fork and using a spatula to transfer them to dessert plates.

ORANGE AND RED ONION SALAD WITH CUMIN VINAIGRETTE*

◆

HOT AND SPICY TURKEY CHILI*

◆

WARM TORTILLAS

◆

VANILLA CUP CUSTARDS*

◆

This is a simple, festive, and very economical meal, ideal for a small midweek supper, and with the added advantage of being easy to double or triple for a crowd. Chili is no more time consuming to make in a large pot, and its flavor only improves if made ahead and reheated. The colorful salad of oranges and red onions looks most impressive when presented on a large platter, and tortillas—either corn or flour—are nice when served rolled into cylinders and stacked in a basket. A rich vanilla custard is the perfect soothing dessert after a spicy meal. If you do it for a larger group, bake the custard in a large, attractive serving dish.

ORANGE AND RED ONION SALAD
WITH CUMIN VINAIGRETTE

Makes 4 servings

CUMIN VINAIGRETTE
2 tablespoons red wine vinegar
½ teaspoon Dijon mustard
¼ teaspoon salt
⅛ teaspoon black pepper
3 tablespoons olive oil
3 tablespoons vegetable oil
¼ teaspoon ground cumin

ORANGE AND ONION SALAD
4 cups thinly sliced iceberg lettuce
3 seedless oranges, peeled and thinly sliced
⅓ cup thinly sliced red onion

1. To make the vinaigrette, combine the vinegar, mustard, salt, and pepper in a jar or small bowl. Whisk in the olive oil, vegetable oil, and cumin.

2. For the salad, spread the lettuce out on a platter. Arrange the oranges over the lettuce and the red onion on top. Drizzle the vinaigrette over the salad just before serving.

HOT AND SPICY TURKEY CHILI

Makes 4 servings

Adjust the spiciness to your taste by using more cayenne and three jalapeños if you like hotter chili.

2 tablespoons vegetable oil
1 pound ground turkey
1 large onion, chopped
2 garlic cloves, minced
1 tablespoon chili powder
¾ teaspoon dried oregano
⅛ teaspoon cayenne, or to taste
1 (14- to 16-ounce) can tomatoes with their juices
1 cup chicken broth
1 (16-ounce) can red or kidney beans, drained
2 to 3 jalapeño peppers, fresh or canned, minced
¼ teaspoon salt
¼ teaspoon black pepper
2 tablespoons chopped cilantro (optional)

1. Heat the oil in a large skillet or pot. Add the ground turkey, onion, and garlic and cook over medium-high heat, stirring frequently to break up lumps of meat, until the

turkey has lost its pink color and is lightly browned, about 8 minutes.

2. Stir in the chili powder, oregano, and cayenne and cook, stirring, for 1 minute. Add the tomatoes and their juices; break up the tomatoes with the side of a spoon. Add the chicken broth, beans, and jalapeños. Simmer, uncovered, over low heat for 30 minutes. Taste and season with additional salt and pepper if needed. Stir in the cilantro just before serving if using.

VANILLA CUP CUSTARDS

Makes 4 servings

1¾ cups whole milk
Pinch of salt
2 whole eggs
2 egg yolks
⅓ cup sugar
1 teaspoon vanilla extract
¼ teaspoon grated nutmeg

(*continued on next page*)

(*continued*)

1. Preheat the oven to 325 degrees. Line a baking dish with a kitchen towel to help insulate the custard cups from the heat.

2. In a small saucepan, heat the milk and salt just until warm.

3. In a bowl, whisk together the eggs, egg yolks, and sugar. Gradually stir in the warm milk and add the vanilla.

4. Pour the custard into four 5- or 6-ounce custard cups or ramekins and dust the tops with nutmeg. Set the cups on the towel in the baking dish and fill about halfway up the sides with hot water. Bake in the center of the oven for 35 to 45 minutes, until a knife inserted about halfway to the center comes out clean. The centers should still be slightly wobbly when shaken gently.

5. Cool the custards on a rack. Serve at room temperature or refrigerate for up to 1 day.

CAPPELLETTI WITH SUN-DRIED TOMATO SAUCE*

◆

SAUTÉED PEPPERS WITH BALSAMIC VINEGAR*

◆

HERBED GARLIC BREAD*

◆

COFFEE ICE CREAM

◆

Sun-dried tomatoes, which are showing up in more and more supermarkets across the country, take an ordinary tomato sauce to a new level of intensity and depth of flavor. This robust sauce, which is smoothed and enriched with cream, is terrific over a cheese filled pasta, such as cappelletti ("little hats"), tortellini, or ravioli. It's also good over ordinary unfilled pasta, such as linguine—but in that case, add a generous sprinkling of Parmesan cheese over the top. Green peppers, sautéed in olive oil and flavored with a splash of balsamic vinegar, are a pleasingly piquant accompaniment, along with slices of warm herbed garlic bread. And for dessert, bittersweet coffee ice cream seems just right.

CAPPELLETTI WITH SUN-DRIED TOMATO SAUCE

Serves 4

3 tablespoons olive oil
1 onion, chopped
2 ounces sun-dried tomatoes, chopped (about
    ½ cup)
1 (28-ounce) can crushed tomatoes in puree
¼ cup dry red or white wine
1½ teaspoons dried basil
½ cup whipping cream or heavy cream
¼ teaspoon black pepper
12 ounces frozen cheese cappelletti or tortellini

1. Heat the olive oil in a large skillet. Add the onion and cook over medium-low heat for about 5 minutes, until softened. Add the sun-dried tomatoes, crushed tomatoes in puree, wine, and basil. Simmer over low heat, partially covered, for 15 minutes.

2. Stir in the cream and pepper and simmer the sauce, uncovered, over medium heat for 10 minutes longer. (The sauce can be made up to a day ahead and refrigerated. Reheat before using.)

3. Cook the pasta in a large pot of boiling salted water according to package directions until *al dente*, tender but firm, 5 to 8 minutes. Drain and serve with the sauce spooned over the top.

SAUTÉED PEPPERS WITH BALSAMIC VINEGAR

Serves 4

1 to 1½ pounds green bell peppers
2 tablespoons olive oil
1 tablespoon balsamic vinegar
¼ teaspoon salt
⅛ teaspoon black pepper

1. Remove the ribs and seeds from the peppers and cut into 1-inch strips.

2. Heat the olive oil in a large skillet. Add the peppers and cook over medium-high heat, stirring frequently, for about 8 minutes, until lightly browned and somewhat softened. Remove the pan from the heat and pour in the vinegar. It will sizzle and evaporate in the hot pan. Season with the salt and pepper and serve warm or at room temperature.

HERBED GARLIC BREAD

Makes 4 servings

Oregano, thyme, or almost any other dried herb could be substituted for the basil here.

2 tablespoons butter
2 tablespoons olive oil
1 garlic clove, crushed through a press
1 tablespoon chopped parsley
1 teaspoon dried basil
1 (8-ounce) loaf Italian bread
¼ teaspoon paprika

1. In a small saucepan, combine the butter, olive oil, garlic, parsley, and basil. Cook over medium heat, stirring, until the butter is melted, about 1 minute.

2. Split the loaf of bread horizontally in half and brush the seasoned butter over both of the cut sides of the bread. Sprinkle with the paprika.

3. Preheat the broiler. Place the bread, cut sides up, on a baking sheet. Broil, about 5 inches from the heat, until the top is bubbly and lightly browned, about 30 to 60 seconds. Cut into slices and serve in a napkin-lined basket.

CUBED SWISS STEAKS WITH CARROT
AND ONION GRAVY*

◆

GARLIC MASHED POTATOES*

◆

STEAMED GREEN BEANS

◆

DOUBLE CHOCOLATE PUDDING*

◆

To make Swiss steak the old-fashioned way, seasoned flour is pounded into round steak or chuck with a mallet or the edge of a plate, and the stew must simmer for an hour or two until the meat is tender. Cubed steak makes a perfect substitution, because the pounding is already done for you —and so efficiently that the meat doesn't need long cooking! This quickened-up version still has lots of nice gravy, though, to go with the garlic mashed potatoes and green beans or another green vegetable. Chocolate pudding, another comfort classic, is made here with cocoa powder. A little chopped semisweet chocolate is also added for a slightly richer, more chocolatey, taste. Hence, its name.

CUBED SWISS STEAKS WITH CARROT AND ONION GRAVY

Makes 4 servings

Note that the canned tomatoes and wine both get added to the skillet after the vegetables are cooked until almost tender. This is because the acid in these ingredients can retard the tenderizing process to a surprising degree.

3 tablespoons all-purpose flour
¼ teaspoon salt
¼ teaspoon black pepper
1 pound cubed steaks (beef chuck or round)
¼ cup vegetable oil
1 large onion, thinly sliced
1 large celery rib, thinly sliced
2 carrots, very thinly sliced
1 large garlic clove, minced
1 teaspoon dried savory
1 teaspoon dried oregano
1 (16-ounce) can stewed tomatoes, with their juices
¾ cup dry red wine or beef broth
2 tablespoons minced parsley (optional)

1. Combine the flour, salt, and pepper on a plate. Lightly coat both sides of the meat with the seasoned flour; shake off any excess. Reserve the remaining seasoned flour to stir into the gravy later.

2. Heat 2 tablespoons of the oil in a large skillet. Add the meat and cook over high heat, turning once, for 1 to 2 minutes per side, until browned. Remove with tongs or a fork to a plate. (Depending upon the skillet size, this may need to be done in two batches. Do not crowd the pan, or the meat will not brown.)

3. Add the remaining 2 tablespoons of oil to the drippings in the pan along with the onion, celery, and carrots. Cook over medium-high heat, stirring, for 2 minutes, until lightly browned. Reduce the heat to low, cover the skillet, and cook for about 10 minutes, until the vegetables are almost tender.

4. Add the garlic and sprinkle the reserved seasoned flour over the vegetables. Cook, stirring, for 1 minute. Add the savory, oregano, tomatoes with their juices, and the wine.

5. Return the meat and any accumulated juices to the pan. Bring to a simmer, cover, and cook over low heat for 20 minutes, or until the meat and vegetables are tender. Stir in the optional parsley and season with additional salt and pepper to taste.

GARLIC MASHED POTATOES

Makes 4 servings

An old-fashioned potato ricer will do a great job mashing here, but to get light, fluffy potatoes, they need to be beaten hard after the warm milk is added. Do not puree in a food processor, though, or you will end up with glue.

1½ to 2 pounds russet or all-purpose potatoes
2 tablespoons butter
1 small garlic clove, crushed through a press
½ cup milk
½ teaspoon salt
¼ teaspoon black pepper

1. Peel the potatoes and cut them into 2-inch chunks. In a medium saucepan of lightly salted boiling water, cook the potatoes until fork-tender, about 20 minutes. Drain the potatoes well and return them to the saucepan. Cook over low heat for 1 minute, tossing, to evaporate remaining moisture.

2. Meanwhile, melt the butter in a small saucepan. Add the garlic and cook over low heat for 1 minute. Add the milk and heat until just warm.

3. Using a potato masher, mash the potatoes in the sauce-pan until they are broken up; or put them through a ricer. Gradually add the warm milk and garlic mixture, beating hard with the masher or using a hand-held electric mixer to complete the task. Beat the potato puree until it is smooth, fluffy, and lump-free. Season with the salt and pepper and serve hot.

Double Chocolate Pudding

Makes 4 servings

⅔ cup sugar
¼ cup unsweetened cocoa powder
2½ tablespoons cornstarch
Pinch of salt
2 cups milk
1 ounce semisweet chocolate, chopped
1 tablespoon butter
1 teaspoon vanilla extract
Whipped cream (optional)

(continued on next page)

(*continued*)

1. In a heavy medium saucepan, whisk together the sugar, cocoa, cornstarch, and salt. Whisk in about half of the milk to make a smooth paste and stir in the rest.

2. Place the saucepan over medium heat and cook, stirring constantly, until the mixture comes to a boil and begins to thicken, about 6 minutes. Continue to cook, stirring, for 1 minute longer, until smooth and very thick.

3. Remove the saucepan from the heat and add the chocolate and butter, stirring until they are both melted. Stir in the vanilla.

4. Pour the pudding into 4 dessert bowls or one larger serving dish. Place a sheet of plastic wrap directly on the surface of the pudding to prevent a skin from forming on top and refrigerate until firm. (This will take about 30 minutes for individual dishes, longer for the large bowl.)

5. Serve plain or topped with the optional whipped cream.

MUSSELS AND GARLIC SPAGHETTI*

ITALIAN BREAD

ESCAROLE SALAD WITH HONEY-ORANGE VINAIGRETTE*

ANISE SUGAR COOKIES*

If you've been uncertain about mussels, this is the time to try them. It used to be that mussels needed to be scrubbed to within an inch of their lives to remove mud and barnacles, but these days, now that they are mostly farm raised, about all they need is a quick rinse and then a haircut—to have their black "beards" pulled off. To go with the wonderful garlicky sauce, offer plenty of crusty Italian bread. The salad of bitter greens has a sweet-tart dressing. In keeping with the slightly Italian theme, anise-flavored sugar cookies make a nice dessert. (If you're not an anise lover, simply leave the flavoring out to make regular sugar cookies.)

MUSSELS AND GARLIC SPAGHETTI

Makes 4 servings

When cleaning mussels, discard any that are extra heavy. They're probably full of mud!

3 dozen (about 3 pounds) mussels
¾ cup dry white wine
1 pound spaghetti
¼ cup plus 2 tablespoons olive oil
1 large onion, chopped
4 garlic cloves, minced
½ teaspoon dried oregano
¼ teaspoon crushed hot pepper flakes
⅓ cup sliced black olives
Salt and black pepper
½ cup chopped parsley

1. Rinse the mussels, scrub if necessary, and pull or cut off their black beards. In a large pot, combine the mussels and the wine. Bring to a boil, cover, reduce the heat, and steam the mussels, stirring them up once, until they open, 5 to 7 minutes. Use a slotted spoon to remove the mussels, allowing the liquid to drip back into the pot. Reserve 8 or 12 mussels in the shell for garnish, but remove the remainder

from their shells. Discard any mussels that do not open. Strain the cooking liquid through a double layer of cheese cloth or a clean kitchen towel and reserve the liquid.

2. Cook the pasta in a large pot of boiling salted water for 9 to 10 minutes, until *al dente,* tender but firm. Drain into a colander.

3. While the pasta is cooking, heat the oil in a large skillet. Add the onion and cook over medium heat for about 3 minutes. Add the garlic, oregano, and hot pepper. Cook, stirring, for 2 minutes. Add the reserved mussel cooking liquid and simmer for 2 minutes. Stir in the shelled mussels and the olives and simmer for a few seconds. Taste and season with salt and pepper as needed.

4. Toss the sauce with the hot cooked pasta, sprinkle the parsley over the top, and garnish with the reserved mussels in their shells.

ESCAROLE SALAD WITH HONEY-ORANGE VINAIGRETTE

Makes 4 servings

2 tablespoons red or white wine vinegar
1 tablespoon orange juice
1 teaspoon honey
½ teaspoon Dijon mustard
¼ teaspoon salt
⅛ teaspoon black pepper
3 tablespoons olive oil
3 tablespoons vegetable oil
½ teaspoon grated orange zest
½ head of escarole or chicory, rinsed, dried, and
    torn into bite-sized pieces (about 7 cups)
½ cup chopped sweet onion, either white or red

1. To make the dressing, combine the vinegar, orange juice, honey, mustard, salt, and pepper in a jar or small bowl. Whisk in the olive oil, vegetable oil, and orange zest.

2. For the salad, combine the escarole and onion in a salad bowl. Drizzle on the dressing and toss to coat the leaves.

Anise Sugar Cookies

Makes about 3 dozen cookies

There will be more than enough cookies for a single meal, but it makes most sense to make a large batch. Store the leftovers in the cookie jar or freeze them for another day.

1¾ cups all-purpose flour
½ teaspoon baking soda
½ teaspoon salt
1½ teaspoons ground anise or 2 teaspoons anise
    seed (see Note)
8 tablespoons (1 stick) butter, softened
1 cup sugar
1 egg
1 teaspoon vanilla extract

1. In a mixing bowl, sift or whisk together the flour, baking soda, salt, and anise.

2. In a mixer bowl, cream the butter and ¾ cup of the sugar until well combined. Add the egg and the vanilla and beat until light and fluffy. With the mixer on low speed, beat in the flour mixture until well blended. Shape the

dough into a flattened disk, wrap in plastic wrap, and chill for at least 30 minutes or overnight.

3. Preheat the oven to 350 degrees. Place the remaining ¼ cup sugar in a shallow dish.

4. Pinch off small pieces of dough and roll into 1-inch balls. Roll the balls in the sugar and place 2 inches apart on lightly greased baking sheets. Bake for 10 to 12 minutes, until the tops are cracked and the cookies are very lightly browned.

5. Cool the cookies on racks. Store in a covered container for 3 days or freeze for 2 weeks.

NOTE: The anise seeds should be crushed or bruised to release their flavor. Use a mortar and pestle, a mini-food processor, or wrap in several thicknesses of plastic wrap and crush with a mallet, a rolling pin, or the bottom of a small heavy pot.

CHICKEN AND VEGETABLE STEW*

◆

SCALLION CORNMEAL DUMPLINGS*

◆

GREEN SALAD

◆

APPLESAUCE HAND CAKE*

◆

Chicken and dumplings sounds as though it could take all afternoon to make, but these days, with boneless chicken parts and good-quality canned chicken broth, it's much easier than pie. The dumplings (really poached biscuits) are made with the addition of a little cornmeal and flecks of green scallion. They're spooned on top of the simmering stew to steam during the last fifteen minutes or so of cooking time, and they help to thicken the broth. These dumplings are also delicious when poached in simmering chicken broth and served as a side dish with plain meat, such as leftover chicken. Serve the stew in wide shallow soup plates with a big salad of dark leafy greens such as spinach or escarole and a simple oil and vinegar dressing. Offer a square of this moist, gently spiced applesauce cake for dessert. It's an old-fashioned recipe, and as its name suggests, it's meant to be picked up and eaten out of hand.

CHICKEN AND VEGETABLE STEW

Makes 4 servings

1 pound skinless, boneless chicken thighs, cut in
   half crosswise
5 cups chicken broth
6 medium carrots, peeled and cut into thin slices
2 celery ribs, sliced
1 medium onion, chopped
1 teaspoon dried leaf or powdered sage
1 bay leaf
Scallion Cornmeal Dumplings (recipe follows;
   optional)
½ teaspoon salt
¼ teaspoon black pepper

1. In a large saucepan, combine the chicken, chicken broth, carrots, celery, onion, sage, and bay leaf. Bring to a simmer, cover, and cook over low heat for 10 minutes.

2. If making the dumplings, add them at this point. Simmer for 20 minutes longer, until the chicken is no longer pink and the vegetables are tender. Season with the salt and black pepper.

SCALLION CORNMEAL DUMPLINGS

Makes 4 servings (about 12 dumplings)

1 cup plus 2 tablespoons all-purpose flour
2 tablespoons cornmeal, preferably yellow
2 teaspoons baking powder
½ teaspoon salt
3 tablespoons minced scallions, including green tops
3 tablespoons chilled solid vegetable shortening or
    butter
½ cup milk

1. In a mixing bowl, combine the flour, cornmeal, baking powder, salt, and scallions, whisking or stirring to mix well. Cut the shortening or butter into about 10 pieces and work it into the flour with your fingertips until the mixture resembles coarse meal. Add the milk and stir just until a soft dough forms.

2. Drop the dough by rounded tablespoons into simmering liquid, making about 12 dumplings. Cover and simmer over low heat for 20 minutes, or until the dumplings are risen and cooked through.

APPLESAUCE HAND CAKE

Makes 9 squares

If you want to gild the lily, serve this cake with a scoop of vanilla ice cream or whipped cream.

   4 tablespoons (½ stick) butter
   ⅔ cup packed light brown sugar
   ⅔ cup unsweetened applesauce
   2 eggs
   1 cup all-purpose flour
   1 teaspoon ground cinnamon
   ½ teaspoon grated nutmeg
   ¾ teaspoon baking powder
   ¼ teaspoon baking soda
   ¼ teaspoon salt
   ¼ cup raisins

1. Preheat the oven to 350 degrees. Butter a 9-inch square baking pan.

2. In a medium saucepan, heat the butter and sugar together over medium heat, stirring, until melted and bubbly. Remove from the heat and stir in the applesauce; then whisk in the eggs until well blended.

3. In a mixing bowl, whisk or sift together the flour, cinnamon, nutmeg, baking powder, baking soda, and salt. Stir in the raisins.

4. Add the dry ingredients to the saucepan and stir or whisk just until blended. Pour the batter into the prepared baking pan.

5. Bake in the center of the oven for 25 minutes, or until the top springs back when lightly touched and a toothpick inserted in the center comes out clean.

6. Let the cake cool in the pan on a rack for at least 10 minutes before cutting into squares. (This recipe can be made several hours ahead. Refrigerate leftovers for 1 to 2 days.)

Index

◆